W0006936

Coaching Youth Football

Third Edition

American Sport Education Program

Human Kinetics

Library of Congress Cataloging-in-Publication Data
Coaching youth football / American Sport Education Program.--3rd ed.
  p. cm.
  ISBN 0-7360-3792-6
  1. Youth league football--Coaching.   I. American Sport Education Program.

GV956.6.R66 2001
796.332'07'7--dc21

2001016875

ISBN: 0-7360-3792-6

Copyright © 2001, 1997, 1993 by Human Kinetics Publishers, Inc.

All rights reserved. Except for use in a review, the reproduction or utilization of this work in any form or by any electronic, mechanical, or other means, now known or hereafter invented, including xerography, photocopying, and recording, and in any information storage and retrieval system, is forbidden without the written permission of the publisher.

Materials in chapter 4 are reprinted, with permission from the YMCA of the USA, 1999, *YMCA Coaching Winners Baseball and Softball*. (Champaign, IL: Human Kinetics).

Acquisitions Editor: Tom Hanlon; **Games Consultant**: Terry Crowther; **Managing Editor**: Wendy McLaughlin; **Assistant Editor**: Dan Brachtesende; **Copyeditor**: Jan Feeney; **Proofreader**: Sue Fetters; **Graphic Designer**: Fred Starbird; **Graphic Artist**: Sandra Meier; **Photo Manager**: Clark Brooks; **Cover Designer**: Jack W. Davis; **Photographer (cover)**: © Rob Skeoch; **Photographer (interior)**: Tom Roberts unless otherwise noted; © Anthony Neste on pages 1, 17, 39, 51, 63, 91, 169; Mary Messenger on pages 9, 33; **Art Manager**: Craig Newsom; **Illustrators**: Tom Janowski and Roberto Sabas; **Printer**: United Graphics

Copies of this book are available at special discounts for bulk purchase for sales promotions, premiums, fund-raising, or educational use. Special editions or book excerpts can also be created to specifications. For details, contact the Special Sales Manager at Human Kinetics.

Printed in the United States of America   10 9 8 7 6 5 4 3 2 1

Human Kinetics
Web site: www.humankinetics.com

United States: Human Kinetics
P.O. Box 5076, Champaign, IL 61825-5076
800-747-4457
e-mail: humank@hkusa.com

Canada: Human Kinetics
475 Devonshire Road Unit 100, Windsor, ON N8Y 2L5
800-465-7301 (in Canada only)
e-mail: orders@hkcanada.com

Europe: Human Kinetics
Units C2/C3 Wira Business Park, West Park Ring Road,
Leeds LS16 6EB, United Kingdom
+44 (0) 113 278 1708
e mail: humank@hkeurope.com

Australia: Human Kinetics
57A Price Avenue, Lower Mitcham, South Australia 5062
08 8277 1555
e-mail: liahka@senet.com.au

New Zealand: Human Kinetics
P.O. Box 105-231, Auckland Central
09-523-3462
e-mail: hkp@ihug.co.nz

Coaching
Youth Football

Contents

Welcome to Coaching!

Coaching young people is an exciting way to be involved in sport. But it isn't easy. Some coaches are overwhelmed by the responsibilities involved in helping athletes through their early sport experiences. And that's not surprising, because coaching youngsters requires more than bringing the balls to the field and letting them play. It involves preparing them physically and mentally to compete effectively, fairly, and safely in their sport, and providing them with a positive role model.

This book will help you meet the challenges *and* experience the many rewards of coaching young athletes. In this book you'll learn how to meet your responsibilities as a coach, communicate well and provide for safety, use a highly effective method—the games approach—to teaching tactics and skills, and learn strategies for coaching on game day. We also provide three sets of season plans to guide you throughout your season.

This book serves as a text for ASEP's Coaching Youth Sport course. If you would like more information about this course or other ASEP courses and resources, please contact us at

ASEP
P.O. Box 5076
Champaign, IL 61825-5076
1-800-747-5698

www.asep.com

Key to Diagrams

defensive player	X
offensive player	O
quarterback	(QB)
running back	(RB)
receiver	(R)
defensive back	▽ DB
movement without ball	⟶
movement with ball	⟹
pass, punt, kick	⇢
coach	[C]
kicker	(K)
punter	(P)

chapter 1

Stepping Into Coaching

If you are like most youth league coaches, you have probably been recruited from the ranks of concerned parents, sport enthusiasts, or community volunteers. Like many rookie and veteran coaches, you probably have had little formal instruction on how to coach. But when the call went out for coaches to assist with the local youth football program, you answered because you like children and enjoy football, and perhaps because you wanted to be involved in a worthwhile community activity.

Your initial coaching assignment may be difficult. Like many volunteers, you may not know everything there is to know about football or about how to work with children. *Coaching Youth Football* will help you learn the basics of coaching football effectively.

To start, let's take a look at what's involved in being a coach. What are your responsibilities? We'll also talk about how to handle the situation when your child is on the team you coach, and we'll examine five tools for being an effective coach.

Your Responsibilities As a Coach

As a football coach, you'll be called upon to do the following:

1. **Provide a safe physical environment.** Playing football holds an inherent risk, but as a coach you're responsible for regularly inspecting the practice and competition fields (see the checklist for facilities and equipment in chapter 6).

2. **Communicate in a positive way.** You'll communicate not only with your players but also with parents, officials, and administrators. Communicate in a way that is positive and that demonstrates you have the best interests of the players at heart. Chapter 2 will help you communicate effectively and positively.

3. **Teach the tactics and skills of football.** We'll show you an innovative "games approach" to teaching and practicing the tactics and skills young athletes need to know—an approach that kids thoroughly enjoy. We ask you to help all players be the best they can be. In chapter 5 we'll show you how to teach football skills, and in chapter 9 we'll provide season plans for 8- to 9-year-olds, 10- to 11-year-olds, and 12- to 14-year-olds, respectively. In chapter 8 we'll provide descriptions of all the skills you'll need to teach.

4. **Teach the rules of football.** We'll ask you to teach your players the rules of football. You'll find the rules in chapter 7.

5. **Direct players in competition.** This includes determining starting lineups and a substitution plan, relating appropriately to officials and to opposing coaches and players, and making tactical decisions during games (see chapter 6). Remember that the focus is not on winning at all costs, but in coaching your kids to compete well, do their best, and strive to win within the rules.

6. **Help your players become fit and value fitness for a lifetime.** We want you to help your players be fit so they can play football safely and successfully. We also want your players to learn to become fit on their own, understand the value of fitness, and enjoy training. Thus, we ask you not to make them do push-ups or run laps for punishment. Make it fun to get fit for football, and make it fun to play football so they'll stay fit for a lifetime.

These are your responsibilities as a coach. But coaching becomes even more complicated when your child is a player on the team you coach. If this is the case, you'll have to take into account your roles as both a coach and a parent, and think about how those roles relate to each other.

Coaching Your Own Child

Many coaches are parents, but the two roles should not be confused. Unlike your role as a parent, as a coach you are responsible not only to yourself and your child, but also to the organization, all the players on the team (including your child), and their parents. Because of this additional responsibility, your behavior on the football field will be different from your behavior at home, and your son or daughter may not understand why.

For example, imagine the confusion of a young boy who is the center of his parents' attention at home but is barely noticed by his father / coach in the sport setting. Or consider the mixed signals received by a young girl whose football skill is constantly evaluated by a mother / coach who otherwise rarely comments on her daughter's activities. You need to explain to your son or daughter your new responsibilities and how they will affect your relationship when coaching.

Take the following steps to avoid problems in coaching your child:

- Ask your child if he wants you to coach the team.
- Explain why you wish to be involved with the team.
- Discuss with your child how your interactions will change when you take on the role of coach at practices or games.
- Limit your coaching behavior to when you are in the coaching role.
- Avoid parenting during practice or game situations, to keep your role clear in your child's mind.
- Reaffirm your love for your child, irrespective of his performance on the football field.

Now let's look at some of the qualities that will help you become an effective coach.

Five Tools of an Effective Coach

Have you purchased the traditional coaching tools—things like whistles, coaching clothes, sport shoes, and a clipboard? They'll help you coach, but to be a successful coach you'll need five other tools that cannot be bought. These tools are available only through self-examination and hard work; they're easy to remember with the acronym COACH:

C – Comprehension

O – Outlook

A – Affection

C – Character

H – Humor

Comprehension

Comprehension of the rules, tactics, and skills of football is required. You must understand the basic elements of the sport. To assist you in learning about the game, we describe rules, tactics, and skills in chapters 7 and 8. We also provide season plans in chapter 9.

To improve your comprehension of football, take the following steps:

- Read the sport-specific section of this book in chapters 7, 8, and 9.
- Consider reading other football coaching books, including those available from the American Sport Education Program (ASEP).
- Contact youth football organizations.
- Attend football clinics.
- Talk with more experienced coaches.
- Observe local college, high school, and youth football games.
- Watch football games on television.

In addition to having football knowledge, you must implement proper training and safety methods so your players can participate with little risk of injury. Even then, injuries may occur. And more often than not, you'll be the first person responding to your players' injuries, so be sure you understand the basic emergency care procedures described in chapter 3. Also, read in that chapter how to handle more serious sport injury situations.

Outlook

This coaching tool refers to your perspective and goals—what you are seeking as a coach. The most common coaching objectives are to (a) have fun, (b) help players develop their physical, mental, and social skills, and (c) win. Thus your outlook involves the priorities you set, your planning, and your vision for the future.

While all coaches focus on competition, we want you to focus on positive competition, keeping the pursuit of victory in perspective by making decisions that first are in the best interest of the players, and second will help to win the game.

So how do you know if your outlook and priorities are in order? Here's a little test for you:

Which situation would you be most proud of?

    a. Knowing that each participant enjoyed playing football.

    b. Seeing that all players improved their football skills.

    c. Winning the league championship.

Which statement best reflects your thoughts about sport?

    a. If it isn't fun, don't do it.

    b. Everyone should learn something every day.

    c. Sport isn't fun if you don't win.

How would you like your players to remember you?

    a. As a coach who was fun to play for.

    b. As a coach who provided a good base of fundamental skills.

    c. As a coach who had a winning record.

Which would you most like to hear a parent of a player on your team say?

    a. Mike really had a good time playing football this year.

    b. Nicole learned some important lessons playing football this year.

    c. Willie played on the first-place football team this year.

Which of the following would be the most rewarding moment of your season?

    a. Having your team not want to stop playing, even after practice is over.

    b. Seeing one of your players finally master the skill of tackling.

    c. Winning the league championship.

Look over your answers. If you most often selected "a" responses, then having fun is most important to you. A majority of "b" answers suggests that skill development is what attracts you to coaching. And if "c" was your most frequent response, winning is tops on your list of coaching priorities. If your priorities are in order, your players' well-being will take precedence over your team's win-loss record every time.

The American Sport Education Program (ASEP) has a motto that will help you keep your outlook in line with the best interests of the kids on your team. It summarizes in four words all you need to remember when establishing your coaching priorities:

Athletes First, Winning Second

This motto recognizes that striving to win is an important, even vital, part of sports. But it emphatically states that no efforts in striving to win should be made at the expense of the athletes' well being, development, and enjoyment.

Take the following actions to better define your outlook:

1. Determine your priorities for the season.
2. Prepare for situations that challenge your priorities.
3. Set goals for yourself and your players that are consistent with those priorities.
4. Plan how you and your players can best attain those goals.
5. Review your goals frequently to be sure that you are staying on track.

Affection

This is another vital tool you will want to have in your coaching kit: a genuine concern for the young people you coach. It involves having a love for kids, a desire to share with them your love and knowledge of football, and the patience and understanding that allow each individual playing for you to grow from his or her involvement in sport.

You can demonstrate your affection and patience in many ways, including these:

- Make an effort to get to know each player on your team.
- Treat each player as an individual.
- Empathize with players trying to learn new and difficult skills.
- Treat players as you would like to be treated under similar circumstances.
- Be in control of your emotions.
- Show your enthusiasm for being involved with your team.
- Keep an upbeat and positive tone in all of your communications.

Character

The fact that you have decided to coach young football players probably means that you think participation in sport is important. But whether or not that participation develops character in your players depends as much on you as it does on the sport itself. How can you build character in your players?

Having good character means modeling appropriate behaviors for sport and life. That means more than just saying the right things. What you say and what you do must match. There is no place in coaching for the "Do as I say, not as I do" philosophy. Challenge, support, encourage, and reward every youngster, and your players will be more likely to accept, even celebrate, their differences. Be in control before, during, and after all practices and contests. And don't be afraid to admit that you were wrong. No one is perfect!

Consider the following steps to being a good role model:

- Take stock of your strengths and weaknesses.
- Build on your strengths.
- Set goals for yourself to improve upon those areas you would not like to see copied.
- If you slip up, apologize to your team and to yourself. You'll do better next time.

Humor

Humor is an often-overlooked coaching tool. For our use it means having the ability to laugh at yourself and with your players during practices and contests. Nothing helps balance the tone of a serious skill-learning session like a chuckle or two. And a sense of humor puts in perspective the many mistakes your players will make. So don't get upset over each miscue or respond negatively to erring players. Allow your players and yourself to enjoy the ups, and don't dwell on the downs.

Here are some tips for injecting humor into your practices:

- Make practices fun by including a variety of activities.
- Keep all players involved in games and skill practices.
- Consider laughter by your players a sign of enjoyment, not of waning discipline.
- Smile!

chapter 2

Communicating As a Coach

In chapter 1 you learned about the tools needed to COACH: Comprehension, Outlook, Affection, Character, and Humor. These are essentials for effective coaching; without them, you'd have a difficult time getting started. But none of the tools will work if you don't know how to use them with your athletes—and this requires skillful communication. This chapter examines what communication is and how you can become a more effective communicator-coach.

What's Involved in Communication?

Coaches often mistakenly believe that communication involves only instructing players to do something, but verbal commands are only a small part of the communication process. More than half of what is communicated is nonverbal. So remember when you are coaching: Actions speak louder than words.

Communication in its simplest form involves two people: a sender and a receiver. The sender transmits the message verbally, through facial expressions, and possibly through body language. Once the message is sent, the receiver must assimilate it successfully. A receiver who fails to attend or listen will miss parts, if not all, of the message.

How Can I Send More Effective Messages?

Young athletes often have little understanding of the rules and skills of football and probably even less confidence in playing it. So they need accurate, understandable, and supportive messages to help them along. That's why your verbal and nonverbal messages are so important.

Verbal Messages

"Sticks and stones may break my bones, but words will never hurt me" isn't true. Spoken words can have a strong and long-lasting effect. And coaches' words are particularly influential because youngsters place great importance on what coaches say. Perhaps you, like many former youth sport participants, have a difficult time remembering much of anything you were told by your elementary school teachers, but you can still recall several specific things your coaches at that level said to you. Such is the lasting effect of a coach's comments to a player.

Whether you are correcting misbehavior, teaching a player how to catch the ball, or praising a player for good effort, you should consider a number of things when sending a message verbally. They include the following:

- Be positive and honest.
- State it clearly and simply.
- Say it loud enough, and say it again.
- Be consistent.

Be Positive and Honest

Nothing turns people off like hearing someone nag all the time, and athletes react similarly to a coach who gripes constantly. Kids particularly need encouragement because they often doubt their ability to perform in a sport. So look for and tell your players what they did well.

But don't cover up poor or incorrect play with rosy words of praise. Kids know all too well when they've erred, and no cheerfully expressed cliche can undo their mistakes. If you fail to acknowledge players' errors, your athletes will think you are a phony.

A good way to correct a performance error is to first point out what the athlete did correctly. Then explain in a positive way what he is doing wrong and show him how to correct it. Finish by encouraging the athlete and emphasizing the correct performance.

Be sure not to follow a positive statement with the word *but.* For example, don't say, "Good hands on that catch, Reggie. But if you'd make better fakes and sharper cuts, you'd get more open than that." Saying it this way causes many kids to ignore the positive statement and focus on the negative one. Instead, say something like, "Good hands on that catch, Reggie. And if you would sell your fakes a little more and make sharper cuts, you'll shake your defender a bit more. Good catch. Way to go."

State It Clearly and Simply

Positive and honest messages are good, but only if expressed directly in words your players understand. "Beating around the bush" is ineffective and inefficient. And if you do ramble, your players will miss the point of your message and probably lose interest. Here are some tips for saying things clearly:

- Organize your thoughts before speaking to your athletes.
- Explain things thoroughly, but don't bore them with long-winded monologues.
- Use language your players can understand. However, avoid trying to be hip by using their age group's slang vocabulary.

Say It Loud Enough, and Say It Again

Talk to your team in a voice that all members can hear and interpret. A crisp, vigorous voice commands attention and respect; garbled and weak speech is tuned out. It's OK, in fact, appropriate, to soften your voice when speaking to a player individually about a personal problem. But most of the time your messages will be for all your players to hear, so make sure they can! An enthusiastic voice also motivates players and tells them you enjoy being their coach. A word of caution, however: Don't dominate the setting with a booming voice that distracts attention from players' performances.

Sometimes what you say, even if stated loudly and clearly, won't sink in the first time. This may be particularly true when young athletes hear words they don't understand. To avoid boring repetition and yet still get your message across, say the same thing in a slightly different way. For instance, you might first tell your players, "Get an angle on the runner." If they don't appear to understand, you might say, "Try to meet and tackle the ball carrier near or behind the line of scrimmage, without letting him get by you for a touchdown." The second form of the message may get through to players who missed it the first time around.

Be Consistent

People often say things in ways that imply a different message. For example, a touch of sarcasm added to the words "Way to go!" sends an entirely different message than the words themselves suggest. Avoid sending such mixed messages. Keep the tone of your voice consistent with the words you use. And don't say something one day and contradict it the next; players will get their wires crossed.

Nonverbal Messages

Just as you should be consistent in the tone of voice and words you use, you should also keep your verbal and nonverbal messages consistent. An extreme example of failing to do this would be shaking your head, indicating disapproval, while at the same time telling a player "Nice try." Which is the player to believe, your gesture or your words?

Messages can be sent nonverbally in a number of ways. Facial expressions and body language are just two of the more obvious forms of nonverbal signals that can help you when you coach.

Facial Expressions

The look on a person's face is the quickest clue to what she thinks or feels. Your players know this, so they will study your face, looking for any sign that will tell them more than the words you say. Don't try to fool them by putting on a happy or blank "mask." They'll see through it, and you'll lose credibility.

Serious, stone-faced expressions are no help to kids who need cues as to how they are performing. They will just assume you're unhappy or disinterested. Don't be afraid to smile. A smile from a coach can give a great boost to an unsure athlete. Plus, a smile lets your players know that you are happy coaching them. But don't overdo it, or your players won't be able to tell when you are genuinely pleased by something they've done or when you are just putting on a smiling face.

Body Language

What would your players think you were feeling if you came to practice slouched over with your head down and shoulders slumped? Tired?

Bored? Unhappy? What would they think you were feeling if you watched them during a contest with your hands on your hips, your jaws clenched, and your face reddened? Upset with them? Disgusted at an official? Mad at a fan? Probably some or all of these things would enter your players' minds. And none of these impressions is the kind you want your players to have of you. That's why you should carry yourself in a pleasant, confident, and vigorous manner. Such a posture not only projects happiness with your coaching role but also provides a good example for your young players, who may model your behavior.

Physical contact can also be a very important use of body language. A handshake, a pat on the head, an arm around the shoulder, or even a big hug are effective ways of showing approval, concern, affection, and joy to your players. Youngsters are especially in need of this type of nonverbal message. Keep within the obvious moral and legal limits, of course, but don't be reluctant to touch your players, sending a message that can only truly be expressed in that way.

How Can I Improve My Receiving Skills?

Now, let's examine the other half of the communication process— receiving messages. Too often very good senders are very poor receivers of messages. But as a coach of young athletes, you must be able to fulfill both roles effectively.

The requirements for receiving messages are quite simple, but receiving skills are perhaps less satisfying and therefore underdeveloped compared to sending skills. People seem to naturally enjoy hearing themselves talk more than hearing others talk. But if you read about the keys to receiving messages and make a strong effort to use them with your players, you'll be surprised by what you've been missing.

Attention!

First, you must pay attention; you must want to hear what others have to communicate to you. That's not always easy when you're busy coaching and have many things competing for your attention. But in one-on-one or team meetings with players, you must really focus on what they are telling you, both verbally and nonverbally. You'll be amazed at the little signals you pick up. Not only will such focused attention help you catch every word your players say, but also you'll notice your players' moods and physical states. In addition, you'll get an idea of your players' feelings toward you and other players on the team.

Listen CARE-FULLY

How we receive messages from others, perhaps more than anything else we do, demonstrates how much we care for the sender and what that person has to tell us. If you care little for your players or have little regard for what they have to say, it will show in how you attend and listen to them. Check yourself. Do you find your mind wandering to what you are going to do after practice while one of your players is talking to you? Do you frequently have to ask your players, "What did you say?" If so, you need to work on your receiving mechanics of attending and listening. But perhaps the most critical question you should ask yourself, if you find that you're missing the messages your players send, is this: Do I care?

Providing Feedback

So far we've discussed separately the sending and receiving of messages. But we all know that senders and receivers switch roles several times during an interaction. One person initiates a communication by sending a message to another person, who then receives the message. The receiver then switches roles and becomes the sender by responding to the person who sent the initial message. These verbal and nonverbal responses are called *feedback*.

Your players will be looking to you for feedback all the time. They will want to know how you think they are performing, what you think of their ideas, and whether their efforts please you. Obviously, you can respond in many different ways. How you respond will strongly affect your players. They will respond most favorably to positive feedback.

Praising players when they have performed or behaved well is an effective way of getting them to repeat (or try to repeat) that behavior in the future. And positive feedback for effort is an especially effective way to motivate youngsters to work on difficult skills. So rather than shouting and providing negative feedback to players who have made mistakes, try offering players positive feedback, letting them know what they did correctly and how they can improve.

Sometimes just the way you word feedback can make it more positive than negative. For example, instead of saying, "Don't run with the ball that way," you might say, "Run with the ball this way." Then your players will be focusing on what to do instead of what not to do.

You can give positive feedback verbally and nonverbally. Telling a player, especially in front of teammates, that she has performed well, is a great way to boost the confidence of a youngster. And a pat on the back or a handshake can be a very tangible way of communicating your recognition of a player's performance.

Who Else Do I Need to Communicate With?

Coaching involves not only sending and receiving messages and providing proper feedback to players, but also interacting with parents, fans, contest officials, and opposing coaches. If you don't communicate effectively with these groups of people, your coaching career will be unpleasant and short-lived. So try the following suggestions for communicating with these groups.

Parents

A player's parents need to be assured that their son or daughter is under the direction of a coach who is both knowledgeable about the sport and concerned about the youngster's well-being. You can put their worries to rest by holding a preseason parent-orientation meeting in which you describe your background and your approach to coaching.

If parents contact you with a concern during the season, listen to them closely and try to offer positive responses. If you need to communicate with parents, catch them after a practice, give them a phone call, or send a note through the mail. Messages sent to parents through players are too often lost, misinterpreted, or forgotten.

Fans

The stands probably won't be overflowing at your contests, but that only means that you'll more easily hear the few fans who criticize your coaching. When you hear something negative said about the job you're doing, don't respond. Keep calm, consider whether the message had any value, and if not, forget it. Acknowledging critical, unwarranted comments from a fan during a contest will only encourage others to voice their opinions. So put away your "rabbit ears" and communicate to fans, through your actions, that you are a confident, competent coach.

Prepare your players for fans' criticisms. Tell them it is you, not the spectators, they should listen to. If you notice that one of your players is rattled by a fan's comment, reassure the player that your evaluation is more objective and favorable—and the one that counts.

Contest Officials

How you communicate with officials will have a great influence on the way your players behave toward them. Therefore, you need to set an example. Greet officials with a handshake, an introduction, and perhaps some casual conversation about the upcoming contest. Indicate your respect for them before, during, and after the contest. Don't make nasty remarks, shout, or use disrespectful body gestures. Your players will see you do it, and they'll get the idea that such behavior is appropriate. Plus, if the official hears or sees you, the communication between the two of you will break down.

Opposing Coaches

Make an effort to visit with the coach of the opposing team before the game. During the game, don't get into a personal feud with the opposing coach. Remember, it's the kids, not the coaches, who are competing. And by getting along well with the opposing coach, you'll show your players that competition involves cooperation.

chapter 3

Providing for Players' Safety

Your fullback breaks free through a huge hole in the line, and it appears he has daylight all the way to the end zone. Suddenly, a linebacker comes from nowhere and makes a crushing tackle on the runner. Although momentarily pleased with the yardage gained on the play, you quickly become concerned when you see that the ball carrier is not getting to his feet. He seems to be in pain. What do you do?

No coach wants to see players get hurt. But injury remains a reality of sport participation; consequently, you must be prepared to provide first aid when injuries occur and to protect yourself against unjustified lawsuits. Fortunately, there are many preventive measures coaches can institute to reduce the risk. In this chapter we describe

⊙ steps you can take to prevent injuries,

⊙ first aid and emergency responses for when injuries occur, and

⊙ your legal responsibilities as a coach.

The Game Plan for Safety

You can't prevent all injuries from happening, but you can take preventive measures that give your players the best possible chance for injury-free participation. In creating the safest possible environment for your athletes, we'll explore what you can do in these six areas:

⊙ Preseason physical examinations

⊙ Physical conditioning

⊙ Equipment and facilities inspection

⊙ Player match-ups and inherent risks

⊙ Proper supervision and record keeping

⊙ Environmental conditions

We'll begin with what should take place *before* the season begins: the preseason physical examination.

Preseason Physical Examination

We recommend that your players have a physical examination before participating in football. The exam should address the most likely areas of medical concern and identify youngsters at high risk. We also suggest that you have players' parents or guardians sign a participation agreement form and a release form to allow their children to be treated in case of an emergency.

Physical Conditioning

Players need to be in, or get in, shape to play the game at the level expected. To do so, they'll need to have adequate *cardiorespiratory fitness* and *muscular fitness.*

Cardiorespiratory fitness involves the body's ability to store and use oxygen and fuels efficiently to power muscle contractions. As players get in better shape, their bodies are able to more efficiently deliver oxygen and fuels to muscles and carry off carbon dioxide and other wastes. Football involves lots of running and exertion; most players will be making short bursts throughout a game. Youngsters who aren't as fit as their peers often overextend in trying to make up for their lack of fitness, which could result in lightheadedness and nausea.

An advantage of teaching football with the games approach is that kids are active during almost the entire practice; there is no standing around in lines, watching teammates take part in drills. Players will be attaining higher levels of cardiorespiratory fitness as the season progresses simply by taking part in practice. However, watch closely for signs of low levels of cardiorespiratory fitness; don't let your athletes do too much until they're fit. You might privately counsel youngsters who appear overly winded, suggesting that they train outside of practice to increase their fitness.

Muscular fitness encompasses strength, muscle endurance, power, speed, and flexibility. This type of fitness is affected by physical maturity, as well as strength training and other types of training. Your players will likely exhibit a relatively wide range of muscular fitness. Those who have greater muscular fitness will be able to run faster and throw harder. They will also sustain fewer muscular injuries, and any injuries that do occur will tend to be more minor in nature. And in case of injury, recovery rate is accelerated in those with higher levels of muscular fitness.

Two other components of fitness and injury prevention are the warm-up and the cool-down. Although young bodies are generally very limber, they, too, can get tight from inactivity. The warm-up should address each muscle group and get the heart rate elevated in preparation for strenuous activity. Have players warm up for 5 to 10 minutes by playing easy games and stretching.

As practice winds down, slow players' heart rates with an easy jog or walk. Then have players stretch for five minutes to help avoid stiff muscles and make them less tight before the next practice or contest.

Equipment and Facilities Inspection

Another way to prevent injuries is to check the quality and fit of the clothes and protective equipment used by your players. Slick-soled, poor fitting, or unlaced football shoes are a knee or ankle injury waiting to happen. Make sure your players' shoes have appropriately sized studs, are the proper size for their feet, and are double-tied to prevent self-inflicted "shoestring tackles." Two pairs of socks are better than one for preventing blisters.

The pants, pads, jerseys, and helmets your players wear will probably be supplied by your local youth sport program. Check the quality of all equipment and uniforms before fitting them to the kids on your team. After distributing good, proper-fitting equipment, show players how to put on every part of their uniforms. Advise them to wear an undershirt beneath their shoulder pads to reduce the chance of skin irritations.

Make certain that each player on the field has a mouthpiece in place at all times. And tell your athletes that the only time their chin straps should be unsnapped is when they are on the sidelines.

For flag and touch football, check the quality of the flags worn by your players to ensure their safety (especially the safety of their hands when pulling a flag).

Remember also to examine regularly the field on which your players practice and play. Remove hazards, report conditions you cannot remedy, and request maintenance as necessary. If unsafe conditions exist, either make adaptations to avoid risk to your players' safety or stop the practice or game until safe conditions have been restored.

Player Match-Ups and Inherent Risks

We recommend you group teams in two-year age ranges if possible. You'll encounter fewer mismatches in physical maturation with narrow age ranges. Even so, two 12-year-old boys might differ by 90 pounds in weight, a foot in height, and three or four years in emotional and intellectual maturity. This presents dangers for the less mature. Whenever possible, match players against opponents of similar size and physical maturity. Such an approach gives smaller, less mature youngsters a better chance to succeed and avoid injury while providing more mature players with a greater challenge. Closely supervise games so that the more mature do not put the less mature at undue risk.

Proper matching helps protect you from certain liability concerns. But you must also warn players of the inherent risks involved in playing football, because "failure to warn" is one of the most successful arguments in lawsuits against coaches. So, thoroughly explain the inherent risks of football, and make sure each player knows, understands, and appreciates those risks.

The preseason parent-orientation meeting is a good opportunity to explain the risks of the sport to both parents and players. It is also a good occasion on which to have both the players and their parents sign waivers releasing you from liability should an injury occur. Such waivers do not relieve you of responsibility for your players' well-being, but they are recommended by lawyers.

Proper Supervision and Record Keeping

To ensure players' safety, you will need to provide both general supervision and specific supervision. *General supervision* is being in the area of activity so that you can see and hear what is happening. You should be

- immediately accessible to the activity and able to oversee the entire activity,
- alert to conditions that may be dangerous to players and ready to take action to protect them, and
- able to react immediately and appropriately to emergencies.

Specific supervision is direct supervision of an activity at practice. For example, you should provide specific supervision when you teach new skills and continue it until your athletes understand the requirements of the activity, the risks involved, and their own ability to perform in light of these risks. You need to also provide specific supervision when you notice either players breaking rules or a change in the condition of your athletes.

As a general rule, the more dangerous the activity, the more specific the supervision required. This suggests that more specific supervision is required with younger and less experienced athletes.

As part of your supervision duty, you are expected to foresee potentially dangerous situations and to be positioned to help prevent them from occurring. This requires that you know football well, especially the rules that are intended to provide for safety. Prohibit dangerous horseplay, and hold practices only under safe weather conditions. These specific supervisory activities, applied consistently, will make the play environment safer for your players and will help protect you from liability if a mishap does occur.

For further protection, keep records of your season plans, practice plans, and players' injuries. Season and practice plans come in handy when you need evidence that players have been taught certain skills, whereas accurate, detailed injury-report forms offer protection against unfounded lawsuits. Ask for these forms from your sponsoring organization (appendix A has a sample injury report form), and hold onto these records for several years so that an "old football injury" of a former player doesn't come back to haunt you.

Environmental Conditions

Most problems due to environmental factors are related to excessive heat or cold, though you should also consider other environmental factors such as severe weather and pollution. A little thought about the potential problems and a little effort to ensure adequate protection for your athletes will prevent most serious emergencies that are related to environmental conditions.

Heat

On hot, humid days the body has difficulty cooling itself. Because the air is already saturated with water vapor (humidity), sweat doesn't evaporate as easily. Therefore, body sweat is a less effective cooling agent, and the body retains extra heat. Hot, humid environments make athletes prone to heat exhaustion and heatstroke (see more on these in "Serious Injuries" on page 29). And if *you* think it's hot or humid, it's worse on the kids—not only because they're more active, but also because youngsters under the age of 12 have a more difficult time than adults regulating their body temperature. To provide for players' safety in hot or humid conditions, take the following preventive measures.

◉ **Monitor weather conditions and adjust practices accordingly.** Figure 3.1 shows the specific air temperatures and humidity percentages that can be hazardous.

◉ **Acclimatize players to exercising in high heat and humidity.** Athletes can make adjustments to high heat and humidity over 7 to 10 days. During this time, hold practices at low to moderate activity levels and give the players water breaks every 20 minutes.

◉ **Switch to light clothing.** Players should wear shorts and white T-shirts.

◉ **Identify and monitor players who are prone to heat illness.** Players who are overweight, heavily muscled, or out of shape will be more

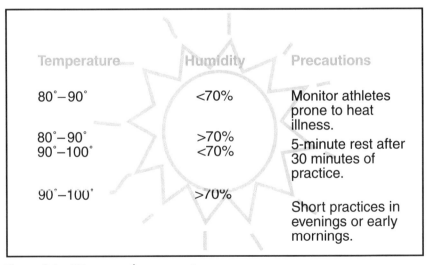

Temperature	Humidity	Precautions
80°–90°	<70%	Monitor athletes prone to heat illness.
80°–90°	>70%	5-minute rest after 30 minutes of practice.
90°–100°	<70%	
90°–100°	>70%	Short practices in evenings or early mornings.

Figure 3.1   Warm-weather precautions.

prone to heat illness, as are athletes who work excessively hard or who have suffered heat illness before. Closely monitor these athletes and give them water breaks every 15 to 20 minutes.

⊙ **Make sure athletes replace water lost through sweat.** Encourage your players to drink one liter of water each day outside of practice and contest times, to drink eight ounces of water every 20 minutes during practice or competition, and to drink four to eight ounces of water 20 minutes before practice or competition.

⊙ **Replenish electrolytes lost through sweat.** Sodium (salt) and potassium are lost through sweat. The best way to replace these nutrients is by eating a normal diet that contains fresh fruits and vegetables. Bananas are a good source of potassium. The normal American diet contains plenty of salt, so players don't need to go overboard in salting their food to replace lost sodium.

Water, Water Everywhere

Encourage players to drink plenty of water before, during, and after practice. Because water makes up 45 percent to 65 percent of a youngster's body weight and water weighs about a pound per pint, the loss of even a little bit of water can have severe consequences for the body's systems. And it doesn't have to be hot and humid for players to become dehydrated. Nor do players have to feel thirsty; in fact, by the time they are aware of their thirst, they are long overdue for a drink.

Cold

When a person is exposed to cold weather, the body temperature starts to drop below normal. To counteract this, the body shivers and reduces the blood flow to gain or conserve heat. But no matter how effective the body's natural heating mechanism is, the body will better withstand cold temperatures if it is prepared to handle them. To reduce the risk of cold-related illnesses, make sure players wear appropriate protective clothing, and keep them active to maintain body heat. Also monitor the windchill (see figure 3.2).

Severe Weather

Severe weather refers to a host of potential dangers, including lightning storms, tornadoes, hail, and heavy rains (which can cause injuries by creating sloppy field conditions).

Temperature (°F)

Wind speed (mph)	0	5	10	15	20	25	30	35	40
40	-55	-45	-35	-30	-20	-15	-5	0	10
35	-50	-40	-35	-30	-20	-10	-5	5	10
30	-50	-40	-30	-25	-20	-10	0	5	10
25	-45	-35	-30	-20	-15	-5	0	10	15
20	-35	-30	-25	-15	-10	0	5	10	20
15	-30	-25	-20	-10	-5	0	10	15	25
10	-20	-15	-10	0	5	10	15	20	30
5	-5	0	5	10	15	20	25	30	35

Flesh may freeze within 1 minute

Windchill temperature (°F)

Figure 3.2 Windchill factor index.

Lightning is of special concern because it can come up quickly and can cause great harm or even kill. For each 5-second count from the flash of lightning to the bang of thunder, lightning is one mile away. A flash-bang of 10 seconds means lightning is two miles away; a flash-bang of 15 seconds indicates lightning is three miles away. A practice or competition should be stopped for the day if lightning is three miles away or less (15 seconds or less from flash to bang).

Safe places in which to take cover when lightning strikes are fully enclosed metal vehicles with the windows up, enclosed buildings, and low ground (under cover of bushes, if possible). It's *not* safe to be near metallic objects—flag poles, fences, light poles, metal bleachers, and so on. Also avoid trees, water, and open fields.

Cancel practice when under either a tornado watch or warning. If for some reason you are practicing or competing when a tornado is nearby, you should get inside a building if possible. If not, lie in a ditch or other low-lying area or crouch near a strong building, and use your arms to protect your head and neck.

The keys to handling severe weather are caution and prudence. Don't try to get that last 10 minutes of practice in if lightning is on the horizon. Don't continue to play in heavy rains. Many storms can strike both quickly and ferociously. Respect the weather and play it safe.

Air Pollution

Poor air quality and smog can present real dangers to your players. Both short- and long-term lung damage are possible from participating in unsafe air. While it's true that participating in clean air is not possible in many areas, restricting activity is recommended when the air-quality ratings are worse than moderate or when there is a smog alert. Your local health department or air-quality control board can inform you of the air-quality ratings for your area and when restricting activities is recommended.

Responding to Players' Injuries

No matter how good and thorough your prevention program is, injuries may occur. When injury does strike, chances are you will be the one in charge. The severity and nature of the injury will determine how actively involved you'll be in treating the injury. But regardless of how seriously a player is hurt, it is your responsibility to know what steps to take. So let's look at how you should prepare to provide basic emergency care to your injured athletes and take the appropriate action when an injury does occur.

Being Prepared

Being prepared to provide basic emergency care involves three steps: being trained in cardiopulmonary resuscitation (CPR) and first aid, having an appropriately stocked first aid kit on hand at practices and games, and having an emergency plan.

CPR and First Aid Training

We recommend that all coaches receive CPR and first aid training from a nationally recognized organization (the National Safety Council, the American Heart Association, the American Red Cross, or the American Sport Education Program). You should be certified based on a practical test and a written test of knowledge. CPR training should include pediatric and adult basic life support and obstructed airway procedures.

First Aid Kit

A well-stocked first aid kit should include the following:

- List of emergency phone numbers
- Change for a pay phone
- Face shield (for rescue breathing and CPR)
- Bandage scissors
- Plastic bags for crushed ice
- 3-inch and 4-inch elastic wraps

- Triangular bandages
- Sterile gauze pads—3-inch and 4-inch squares
- Saline solution for eyes
- Contact lens case
- Mirror
- Penlight
- Tongue depressors
- Cotton swabs
- Butterfly strips
- Bandage strips—assorted sizes
- Alcohol or peroxide
- Antibacterial soap
- First aid cream or antibacterial ointment
- Petroleum jelly
- Tape adherent and tape remover
- $1\frac{1}{2}$-inch white athletic tape
- Prewrap
- Sterile gauze rolls
- Insect sting kit
- Safety pins
- $\frac{1}{8}$-inch, $\frac{1}{4}$-inch, and $\frac{1}{2}$-inch foam rubber
- Disposable surgical gloves
- Thermometer

Emergency Plan

An emergency plan is the final step in preparing to take appropriate action for severe or serious injuries. The plan calls for three steps:

1. **Evaluate the injured player.** Your CPR and first aid training will guide you here.

2. **Call the appropriate medical personnel.** If possible, delegate the responsibility of seeking medical help to another calm and responsible adult who is on hand for all practices and games. Write out a list of emergency phone numbers and keep it with you at practices and games. Include the following phone numbers:

   - Rescue unit
   - Hospital

⊙ Physician

⊙ Police

⊙ Fire department

Take each athlete's emergency information to every practice and game (see appendix B). This information includes the person to contact in case of an emergency, what types of medications the athlete is using, what types of drugs she is allergic to, and so on.

Give an emergency response card (see appendix C) to the contact person calling for emergency assistance. This provides the information the contact person needs to convey and will help keep the person calm, knowing that everything she needs to communicate is on the card. Also complete an injury report form (see appendix A) and keep it on file for any injury that occurs.

3. **Provide first aid.** If medical personnel are not on hand at the time of the injury, you should provide first aid care to the extent of your qualifications. Again, while your CPR and first aid training will guide you here, the following are important guidelines:

⊙ Do not move the injured athlete if the injury is to the head, neck, or back; if a large joint (ankle, knee, elbow, shoulder) is dislocated; or if the pelvis, a rib, or an arm or leg is fractured.

⊙ Calm the injured athlete and keep others away from him or her as much as possible.

⊙ Evaluate whether the athlete's breathing is stopped or irregular, and if necessary, clear the airway with your fingers.

⊙ Administer artificial respiration if the athlete's breathing has stopped. Administer CPR if the athlete's circulation has stopped.

⊙ Remain with the athlete until medical personnel arrive.

Emergency Steps

Your emergency plan should follow this sequence:

1. Check the athlete's level of consciousness.
2. Send a contact person to call the appropriate medical personnel and to call the athlete's parents.
3. Send someone to wait for the rescue team and direct them to the injured athlete.
4. Assess the injury.
5. Administer first aid.
6. Assist emergency medical personnel in preparing the athlete for transportation to a medical facility.

7. Appoint someone to go with the athlete if the parents are not available. This person should be responsible, calm, and familiar with the athlete. Assistant coaches or parents are best for this job.

8. Complete an injury report form while the incident is fresh in your mind (see appendix A).

Taking Appropriate Action

Proper CPR and first aid training, a well-stocked first aid kit, and an emergency plan help prepare you to take appropriate action when an injury occurs. We spoke in the previous section about the importance of providing first aid *to the extent of your qualifications.* Don't "play doctor" with injuries; sort out minor injuries that you can treat from those for which you need to call for medical assistance.

Next we'll look at taking the appropriate action for minor injuries and more serious injuries.

Minor Injuries

Although no injury seems minor to the person experiencing it, most injuries are neither life-threatening nor severe enough to restrict participation. When such injuries occur, you can take an active role in their initial treatment.

Scrapes and Cuts. When one of your players has an open wound, the first thing you should do is put on a pair of disposable surgical gloves or some other effective blood barrier. Then follow these four steps:

1. *Stop the bleeding* by applying direct pressure with a clean dressing to the wound and elevating it. The player may be able to apply this pressure while you put on your gloves. Do not remove the dressing if it becomes soaked with blood. Instead, place an additional dressing on top of the one already in place. If bleeding continues, elevate the injured area above the heart and maintain pressure.

2. *Cleanse the wound* thoroughly once the bleeding is controlled. A good rinsing with a forceful stream of water, and perhaps light scrubbing with soap, will help prevent infection.

3. *Protect the wound* with sterile gauze or a bandage strip. If the player continues to participate, apply protective padding over the injured area.

4. *Remove and dispose of gloves* carefully to prevent you or anyone else from coming into contact with blood.

For bloody noses not associated with serious facial injury, have the athlete sit and lean slightly forward. Then pinch the player's nostrils shut. If the bleeding continues after several minutes, or if the athlete has a history of nosebleeds, seek medical assistance.

Treating Bloody Injuries

You shouldn't let a fear of acquired immune deficiency syndrome (AIDS) stop you from helping a player. You are only at risk if you allow contaminated blood to come in contact with an open wound, so the surgical disposable gloves that you wear will protect you from AIDS should one of your players carry this disease. Check with your director or your organization for more information about protecting yourself and your participants from AIDS.

Strains and Sprains. The physical demands of football practices and games often result in injury to the muscles or tendons (strains) or to the ligaments (sprains). When your players suffer minor strains or sprains, immediately apply the PRICE method of injury care:

P – Protect the athlete and injured body part from further danger or trauma.

R – Rest the area to avoid further damage and foster healing.

I – Ice the area to reduce swelling and pain.

C – Compress the area by securing an ice bag in place with an elastic wrap.

E – Elevate the injury above heart level to keep the blood from pooling in the area.

Bumps and Bruises. Inevitably, football players make contact with each other and with the ground. If the force applied to a body part at impact is great enough, a bump or bruise will result. Many players continue playing with such sore spots, but if the bump or bruise is large and painful, you should act appropriately. Use the PRICE method for injury care and monitor the injury. If swelling, discoloration, and pain have lessened, the player may resume participation with protective padding; if not, the player should be examined by a physician.

Serious Injuries

Head, neck, and back injuries; fractures; and injuries that cause a player to lose consciousness are among a class of injuries that you cannot and should not try to treat yourself. In these cases you should follow the emergency plan outlined on page 26. We do want to examine more closely your role, however, in preventing and handling two heat illnesses: heat exhaustion and heatstroke.

Heat Exhaustion. Heat exhaustion is a shocklike condition caused by dehydration and electrolyte depletion. Symptoms include headache, nausea, dizziness, chills, fatigue, and extreme thirst. Profuse sweating is a key sign of heat exhaustion. Other signs include pale, cool, and clammy skin; rapid, weak pulse; loss of coordination; and dilated pupils. See figure 3.3 for signs and symptoms of heat exhaustion.

A player suffering from heat exhaustion should rest in a cool, shaded area; drink cool water; and have ice applied to the neck, back, or abdomen to help cool the body. You may have to administer CPR if necessary or send for emergency medical assistance if the athlete doesn't recover or his or her condition worsens. Under no conditions should the athlete return to activity that day or before he regains all the weight lost through sweat. If the player has to see a physician, he shouldn't return to the team until he has a written release from the physician.

Heatstroke. Heatstroke is a life-threatening condition in which the body stops sweating and body temperature rises dangerously high. It occurs when dehydration causes a malfunction in the body's temperature control center in the brain. Symptoms include the feeling of being on fire (extremely hot), nausea, confusion, irritability, and fatigue. Signs include hot, dry, and flushed or red skin (this is a key sign); lack of sweat; rapid pulse; rapid breathing; constricted pupils; vomiting; diarrhea; and possibly seizures, unconsciousness, or respiratory or cardiac arrest. See figure 3.3 for signs and symptoms of heatstroke.

Send for emergency medical assistance immediately and have the player rest in a cool, shaded area. Remove excess clothing and equipment from the player, and cool the player's body with cool, wet towels or by pouring cool water over him or her. Apply ice packs to the armpits, neck, back, abdomen, and between the legs. If the player is conscious, have him or her drink cool water. If the player is unconscious, place the player on his or her side to allow fluids and vomit to drain from the mouth.

An athlete who has suffered heatstroke may not return to the team until she has a written release from a physician.

Protecting Yourself

When one of your players is injured, naturally your first concern is the player's well-being. Your feelings for youngsters, after all, are what made

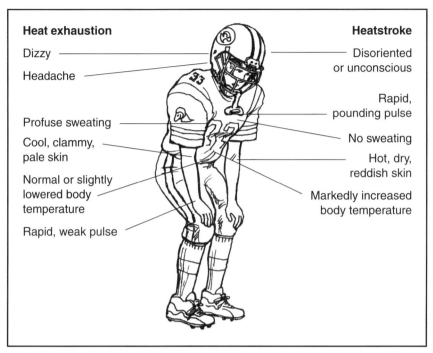

Heat exhaustion

Dizzy

Headache

Profuse sweating

Cool, clammy, pale skin

Normal or slightly lowered body temperature

Rapid, weak pulse

Heatstroke

Disoriented or unconscious

Rapid, pounding pulse

No sweating

Hot, dry, reddish skin

Markedly increased body temperature

Figure 3.3   Signs and symptoms of heat exhaustion and heatstroke.

you decide to coach. Unfortunately, there is something else that you must consider: Can you be held liable for the injury?

From a legal standpoint, a coach has nine duties to fulfill. We've discussed all but planning in this chapter. The following is a summary of your legal duties:

1. Provide a safe environment.
2. Properly plan the activity.
3. Provide adequate and proper equipment.
4. Match, or equate, athletes.
5. Warn of inherent risks in the sport.
6. Supervise the activity closely.
7. Evaluate athletes for injury or incapacitation.
8. Know emergency procedures and first aid.
9. Keep adequate records.

Keep records of your season plan and practice plans and of players' injuries. Season and practice plans come in handy when you need evidence that players have been taught certain skills, and injury reports offer protection against unfounded lawsuits. Hold onto these records for several years so that an "old injury" of a former player doesn't come back to haunt you.

In addition to fulfilling these nine legal duties, you should check your organization's insurance coverage and your insurance coverage to make sure these policies will protect you from liability.

chapter 4

The Games Approach to Coaching Football

Do you remember how as a kid you were taught by adults to play a sport, either in an organized sport program or physical education class? They probably taught you the basic skills using a series of drills that, if the truth be known, you found very boring. As you began to learn the basic skills, they eventually taught you the tactics of the game, showing you when to use these skills in various game situations. Do you remember how impatient you became during what seemed to be endless instruction, and how much you just wanted to play? Well, forget this traditional approach to teaching sports.

Now can you recall learning a sport by playing with a group of your friends in the neighborhood? You didn't learn the basic skills first; no time for that. You began playing immediately. If you didn't know the basic things to do, your friends told you quickly during the game so they could keep playing. Try to remember, because we're going to ask you to use a very similar approach to teaching football to young people called the games approach, an approach we think knocks the socks off the traditional approach.

On the surface, it would seem to make sense to introduce football by first teaching the basic skills of the sport and then the tactics of the game, but we've discovered that this approach has disadvantages. First, it teaches the skills of the sport out of the context of the game. Kids may learn to pass, receive, kick, block, and tackle, but they find it difficult to use these skills in the real game. This is because they do not yet understand the fundamental tactics of football and do not appreciate how best to use their newfound skills.

Second, learning skills by doing drills outside of the context of the game is so-o-o-o boring. The single biggest turnoff about adults teaching kids sports is that we overorganize the instruction and deprive kids of their intrinsic desire to play the game.

As a coach we're asking that you teach football the games approach way. Clear the traditional approach out of your mind. Once you fully understand the games approach, you'll quickly see its superiority in teaching football. Not only will kids learn the game better, but you and your players will have much more fun. And as a bonus, you'll have far fewer discipline problems.

With the games approach to teaching football, we begin with a game. This will be a modified and much smaller game designed to suit the age and ability of the players. As the kids play in these "mini" games, you can begin to help them understand the nature of the game and to appreciate simple concepts of positioning and tactics. When your players understand what they must do in the game, they are then eager to develop the skills to play the game. Now that players are motivated to learn the skills, you can demonstrate the skills of the game, practice using game-like drills, and provide individual instruction by identifying players' errors and helping to correct them.

In the traditional approach to teaching sports, players do this:

Learn the skill → **Learn the tactics** → **Play the game**

In the games approach players do this:

Play the game → **Learn the tactics** → **Learn the skill**

In the past we have placed too much emphasis on the learning of skills and not enough on learning how to play skillfully—that is, how to use those skills in competition. The games approach, in contrast, emphasizes learning what to do first, then how to do it. Moreover— and this is a really important point—the games approach lets kids discover what to do in the game not by you telling them, but by their experiencing it. What you do as an effective coach is help them discover what they've experienced.

In contrast to the "skill-drill-kill the enthusiasm" approach, the games approach is a guided discovery method of teaching. It empowers your kids to solve the problems that arise in the game, and that's a big part of the fun in learning a game.

Now let's look more closely at the games approach to see the four-step process for teaching football:

1. Play a modified football game.
2. Help the players discover what they need to do to play the game successfully.
3. Teach the skills of the game.
4. Practice the skills in another game.

Step 1. Play a Modified Football Game

Okay, it's the first day of practice; some of the kids are eager to get started, while others are obviously apprehensive. Some have rarely thrown a ball, most don't know the rules, and none knows the positions in football. What do you do?

If you use the traditional approach, you start with a little warm-up activity, then line the players up for a simple receiving drill and go from there. With the games approach, you begin by playing a modified game that is developmentally appropriate for the level of the players and also designed to focus on learning a specific part of the game.

Modifying the game emphasizes a limited number of situations in the game. This is one way you "guide" your players to discover certain tactics in the game.

For instance, you have your players play 2 v 1 games in 5-square-yard areas. The objective of the game is for the offensive line player to protect the quarterback for five seconds, not allowing the defender to touch the quarterback within that period (and not allowing the quarterback to run outside the playing area). Playing the game this way forces the line player to think about what he has to do to protect the quarterback.

Step 2. Help the Players Discover What They Need to Do

As your players are playing the game, look for the right spot to "freeze" the action, step in, and hold a brief question-and-answer session to discuss problems they were having in carrying out the goals of the game. You don't need to pop in on the first miscue, but if they repeat the same types of mental or physical mistakes a few times in a row, step in and ask them questions that relate to the aim of the game and the necessary skills required. The best time to interrupt the game is when you notice that they are having trouble carrying out the main goal, or aim, of the game. By stopping the game, freezing action, and asking questions, you'll help them understand

- what the aim of the game is,
- what they must do to achieve that aim, and
- what skills they must use to achieve that aim.

For example, your players are playing a game in which the objective is to protect the quarterback, but they are having trouble doing so. Interrupt the action and ask the following questions:

Coach: What are you supposed to do in this game?

Players: Protect the quarterback.

Coach: What do you have to do to do that?

Players: Get in good position to block.

Coach: Yes, and what else?

Players: Use good technique in blocking.

Coach: OK. You have to be able to get in good position to block and use good technique. Why don't we practice pass protection blocking?

Through the modified game and skillful questioning on your part, your players realize that pass protection blocking is crucial to executing a successful offense. Just as important, rather than *telling* them that pass protection blocking is critical, you led them to that discovery through a well-designed modified game and through questions. This questioning that leads to players' discovery is a crucial part of the games approach. Essentially you'll be asking your players—usually literally— "What do you need to do to succeed in this situation?"

Asking the right questions is a very important part of your teaching. At first asking questions will be difficult because your players have little or no experience with the game. And if you've learned sport through the traditional approach, you'll be tempted to tell your players how to play the game and not waste time asking them questions. Resist this powerful temptation to tell them what to do, and especially don't do so before they begin to play the game.

If your players have trouble understanding what to do, phrase your questions to let them choose between one option versus another. For example, if you ask them "What's the fastest way to get the ball down the field?" and get answers such as "Kick it," then ask, "Is it passing or running the ball?"

Immediately following the question-and-answer session you will begin a skill practice, which is Step 3 of the four-step process.

Sometimes players simply need to have more time playing the game, or you may need to modify the game further so that it is even easier for them to discover what they are to do. It'll take more patience on your part, but it's a powerful way to learn.

Step 3. Teach the Skills of the Game

Only when your players recognize the skills they need to be successful in the game do you want to teach the specific skills through focused drills. This is when you use a more traditional approach to teaching sport skills, the "IDEA" approach, which we will describe in chapter 5.

Step 4. Practice the Skills in Another Game

Once the players have practiced the skill, you then put them in another game situation to let them practice the skill in the context of a game.

We recommend that you typically use even-sided games in Game 1s and lopsided games in Game 2s. By "even-sided" we mean 2 v 2 or 3 v 3, though keep in mind if you're playing a passing game and no one is rushing the quarterback, then an "even-sided" game would be 3 v 2, as this would pit two receivers against two defensive backs. The reasoning behind this is to introduce players to a situation similar to what they will experience in competition, and to let them discover the challenges they face in performing the necessary skill. Then you teach them the skill, have them practice it, and put them back in another game—this time a lopsided one to give them a greater chance of experiencing success.

And that's the games approach. Your players will get to *play* more in practice, and once they learn how the skills fit into their performance and enjoyment of the game, they'll be more motivated to work on those skills, which will help them to be successful.

chapter 5

Teaching and Shaping Skills

Coaching football is about teaching tactics, skills, fitness, values, and other useful things. It's also about "coaching" players before, during, and after contests. Teaching and coaching are closely related, but there are important differences. In this chapter we'll focus on principles of teaching, especially on teaching football skills. But many of the principles we'll discuss apply to teaching tactics, fitness concepts, and values as well. (Most of the other important teaching principles deal with communication, covered in chapter 2.) Then in chapter 6 we'll discuss the principles of coaching, which refer to your leadership activities during contests.

Teaching Football Skills

Many people believe that the only qualification needed to teach a skill is to have performed it. It's helpful to have performed it, but there is much more than that to teaching successfully. And even if you haven't performed the skill before, you can still learn to teach successfully with the useful acronym IDEA:

I – Introduce the skill.

D – Demonstrate the skill.

E – Explain the skill.

A – Attend to players practicing the skill.

These are the basic steps of good teaching. Now we'll explain each step in greater detail.

Introduce the Skill

Players, especially young and inexperienced ones, need to know what skill they are learning and why they are learning it. You should therefore take these three steps every time you introduce a skill to your players:

1. Get your players' attention.
2. Name the skill.
3. Explain the importance of the skill.

Get Your Players' Attention

Because youngsters are easily distracted, use some method to get their attention. Some coaches use interesting news items or stories. Others use jokes. And still others simply project enthusiasm to get their players to listen. Whatever method you use, speak slightly above the normal volume and look your players in the eye when you speak.

Also, position players so they can see and hear you. Arrange the players in two or three evenly spaced rows, facing you. (Make sure they aren't looking into the sun or at some distracting activity.) Then ask if all of them can see you before you begin.

Name the Skill

Although you might mention other common names for the skill, decide which one you'll use and stick with it. This will help avoid confusion and enhance communication among your players.

Explain the Importance of the Skill

Although the importance of a skill may be apparent to you, your players may be less able to see how the skill will help them become better football players. Offer them a reason for learning the skill and describe how the skill relates to more advanced skills.

> *The most difficult aspect of coaching is this: Coaches must learn to let athletes learn. Sport skills should be taught so they have meaning to the child, not just meaning to the coach.*
>
> —Rainer Martens,
> founder of the American Sport Education Program

Demonstrate the Skill

The demonstration step is the most important part of teaching sport skills to players who may never have done anything closely resembling the skill. They need a picture, not just words. They need to see how the skill is performed.

If you are unable to perform the skill correctly, have an assistant coach, one of your players, or someone else more skilled perform the demonstration. These tips will help make your demonstrations more effective:

- Use correct form.
- Demonstrate the skill several times.
- Slow down the action, if possible, during one or two performances so players can see every movement involved in the skill.
- Perform the skill at different angles so your players can get a full perspective of it.
- Demonstrate the skill with both the right and the left arms or legs.

Explain the Skill

Players learn more effectively when they're given a brief explanation of the skill along with the demonstration. Use simple terms and, if possible, relate the skill to previously learned skills. Ask your players whether they understand your description. A good technique is to ask the team to repeat your explanation. Ask questions like "What are you going to do first?" and "Then what?" Should players look confused or uncertain, repeat your explanation and demonstration. If possible, use different words so your players get a chance to try to understand the skill from a different perspective.

Complex skills often are better understood when they are explained in more manageable parts. For instance, if you want to teach your players how to provide pass protection blocking, you might take the following steps:

1. Show them a correct performance of the entire skill, and explain its function in football.
2. Break down the skill and point out its component parts to your players.
3. Have players perform each of the component skills you have already taught them, such as proper body position, delivering a blow to stop the defensive charge, and proper footwork.
4. After players have demonstrated their ability to perform the separate parts of the skill in sequence, reexplain the entire skill.
5. Have players practice the skill in game-like conditions.

One caution: Young players have short attention spans, and a long demonstration or explanation of the skill will bore them. So spend no more than a few minutes altogether on the introduction, demonstration, and explanation phases. Then get the players active in a game that calls on them to perform the skill. The total IDEA should be completed in 10 minutes or less, followed by games in which players practice the skill.

Attend to Players Practicing the Skill

If the skill you selected was within your players' capabilities and you have done an effective job of introducing, demonstrating, and explaining it, your players should be ready to attempt the skill. Some players may need to be physically guided through the movements during their first few attempts. Walking unsure athletes through the skill in this way will help them gain confidence to perform the skill on their own.

Your teaching duties don't end when all your athletes have demonstrated that they understand how to perform the skill. In fact, a significant part of your teaching will involve observing closely the hit-and-miss trial performances of your players. In the next section we'll guide you in shaping players' skills, and then we'll help you learn how to detect and correct errors, using positive feedback. Keep in mind that your feedback will have a great influence on your players' motivation to practice and improve their performances.

Remember, too, that players need individual instruction. So set aside a time before, during, or after practice to give individual help.

Helping Players Improve Skills

After you have successfully taught your players the fundamentals of a skill, your focus will be on helping them improve that skill. Players will learn skills and improve upon them at different rates, so don't get too frustrated. Instead, help them improve by shaping their skills and detecting and correcting errors.

Shaping Players' Skills

One of your principal teaching duties is to reward positive behavior—in terms of successful skill execution—when you see it. A quarterback makes a good pass in practice, and you immediately say, "That's the way to do it! Good follow through!" This, plus a smile and a "thumbs-up" gesture, go a long way toward reinforcing that technique in that player.

However, sometimes you may have a long, dry spell before you have any correct technique to reinforce. It's difficult to reward players when they aren't executing skills correctly. How can you shape their skills if this is the case?

Shaping skills takes practice on your players' part and patience on your part. Expect your players to make errors. Telling the player who made the great pass that he did a good job doesn't ensure that he'll make that pass the next time. Seeing inconsistency in your players' techniques can be frustrating. It's even more challenging to stay positive when your athletes repeatedly perform a skill incorrectly or lack enthusiasm for learning. It can certainly be frustrating to see athletes who seemingly don't heed your advice and continue to make the same mistakes. And when the athletes don't seem to care, you may wonder why you should.

Please know that it is normal to get frustrated at times when teaching skills. Nevertheless, part of successful coaching is controlling this frustration. Instead of getting upset, use these six guidelines for shaping skills:

1. **Think small initially.** Reward the first signs of behavior that approximate what you want. Then reward closer and closer approximations of the desired behavior. In short, use your reward power to shape the behavior you seek.

2. **Break skills into small steps.** For instance, in learning to pass protect block, one of your players does well in his initial move and setup, but he's standing too straight up and not getting into good position. Thus defenders are able to more easily move around him. Reinforce the correct technique used in his initial move and setup, and teach him how to keep his head up and his rear end down. When he masters that, focus on getting him to keep his feet about shoulder-width apart. By doing these things he will be in much better position to block.

3. **Develop one component of a skill at a time.** Don't try to shape two components of a skill at once. For example, in dropping back to throw a pass, quarterbacks must first secure the snap from the center and then use one of the drops—the crossover, the backpedal, or the rollout. Players should focus first on one aspect (receiving the snap from center, using good hand positioning and presenting a good target for the center), then on the other (dropping back, using one of the techniques just mentioned). Athletes who have problems mastering a skill often do so because they're trying to improve two or more components at once. Help these athletes to isolate a single component.

4. **As athletes become more proficient at a skill, reinforce them only occasionally and only for the best examples of the skill behavior.** By focusing only on the best examples, you will help them continue to improve once they've mastered the basics.

5. **When athletes are trying to master a new skill, temporarily relax your standards for how you reward them.** As they focus on the new skill or attempt to integrate it with other skills, the old, well-learned skills may temporarily degenerate.

6. **If, however, a well-learned skill degenerates for long, you may need to restore it by going back to the basics.**

Coaches often have more skilled players provide feedback to teammates as they practice skills. This can be effective, but proceed with caution: You must tell the skilled players exactly what to look for when their teammates are performing the skills. You must also tell them the corrections for the common errors of that skill.

We've looked at how to guide your athletes as they learn skills. Now let's look at another critical teaching principle that you should employ as you're shaping skills: detecting and correcting errors.

Detecting and Correcting Errors

Good coaches recognize that athletes make two types of errors: learning errors and performance errors. *Learning errors* are ones that occur because athletes don't know how to perform a skill; that is, they have not yet developed the correct motor program in the brain to perform a particular skill. *Performance errors* are made not because athletes don't know how to do the skill, but because they made a mistake in executing what they do know. There is no easy way to know whether a player is making learning or performance errors. Part of the art of coaching is being able to sort out which type of error each mistake is.

The process of helping your athletes correct errors begins with your observing and evaluating their performances to determine if the mistakes are learning or performance errors. For performance errors, you need to look for the reasons that your athletes are not performing as well as they know how. If the mistakes are learning errors, then you need to help them learn the skill, which is the focus of this section.

There is no substitute for knowing skills well in correcting learning errors. The better you understand a skill—not only how it is done correctly but also what causes learning errors—the more helpful you will be in correcting mistakes.

One of the most common coaching mistakes is to provide inaccurate feedback and advice on how to correct errors. Don't rush into error correction; wrong feedback or poor advice will hurt the learning process more than no feedback or advice. If you are uncertain about the cause of the problem or how to correct it, continue to observe and analyze until you are more sure. As a rule, you should see the error repeated several times before attempting to correct it.

Correct One Error at a Time

Suppose Michael, one of your punters, is having trouble with punting. He's doing some things well, but you notice that he's not dropping the ball parallel to the ground, and he's not contacting the center of the ball. What do you do?

First, decide which error to correct first, because athletes learn more effectively when they attempt to correct one error at a time. Determine whether one error is causing the other; if so, have the athlete correct that error first, because it may eliminate the other error. In Michael's case, however, neither error is causing the other. In such cases, athletes should correct the error that will bring the greatest improvement when remedied—for Michael, this probably means contacting the center of the ball. Improvement here will likely motivate him to correct the other error.

Use Positive Feedback to Correct Errors

The positive approach to correcting errors includes emphasizing what to do instead of what not to do. Use compliments, praise, rewards, and encouragement to correct errors. Acknowledge correct performance as well as efforts to improve. By using the positive approach, you can help your athletes feel good about themselves and promote a strong desire to achieve.

When you're working with one athlete at a time, the positive approach to correcting errors includes four steps:

1. Praise effort and correct performance.
2. Give simple and precise feedback to correct errors.

3. Make sure the athlete understands your feedback.

4. Provide an environment that motivates the athlete to improve.

Let's take a brief look at each step.

Step 1: Praise Effort and Correct Performance. Praise your athlete for trying to perform a skill correctly and for performing any parts of it correctly. Praise the athlete immediately after she performs the skill, if possible. Keep the praise simple: "Good try," "Way to hustle," or "Good form," "That's the way to follow through." You can also use nonverbal feedback, such as smiling, clapping your hands, or any facial or body expression that shows approval.

Make sure you're sincere with your praise. Don't indicate that an athlete's effort was good when it wasn't. Usually an athlete knows when he has made a sincere effort to perform the skill correctly and perceives undeserved praise for what it is—untruthful feedback to make him feel good. Likewise, don't indicate that a player's performance was correct when it wasn't.

Step 2: Give Simple and Precise Feedback to Correct Errors. Don't burden a player with a long or detailed explanation of how to correct an error. Give just enough feedback so the player can correct one error at a time. Before giving feedback, recognize that some athletes will readily accept it immediately after the error; others will respond better if you slightly delay the correction.

For errors that are complicated to explain and difficult to correct, try the following:

- Explain and demonstrate what the athlete should have done. Do not demonstrate what the athlete did wrong.
- Explain the cause or causes of the error, if this isn't obvious.
- Explain why you are recommending the correction you have selected, if it's not obvious.

Step 3: Make Sure the Athlete Understands Your Feedback. If the athlete doesn't understand your feedback, she won't be able to correct the error. Ask her to repeat the feedback and to explain and demonstrate how it will be used. If the athlete can't do this, be patient and present your feedback again. Then have the athlete repeat the feedback after you're finished.

Step 4: Provide an Environment That Motivates the Athlete to Improve. Your players won't always be able to correct their errors immediately even if they do understand your feedback. Encourage them to "hang tough" and stick with it when corrections are difficult or they seem discouraged. For more difficult corrections, remind them that it will take time, and the improvement will happen only if they work at it. Look to encourage players with low self-confidence. Saying something like, "You were catching much better today; with practice, you'll be able to watch the ball into your hands and catch all of them," can motivate a player to continue to refine his or her receiving skills.

Some athletes need to be more motivated to improve. Others may be very self-motivated and need little help from you in this area at all; with them you can practically ignore Step 4 when correcting an error. While motivation comes from within, look to provide an environment of positive instruction and encouragement to help your athletes improve.

A final note on correcting errors: Team sports such as football provide unique challenges in this endeavor. How do you provide individual feedback in a group setting using a positive approach? Instead of yelling across the field to correct an error (and embarrassing the player), substitute for the player who erred. Then make the correction on the sidelines. This type of feedback has three advantages:

- The player will be more receptive to the one-on-one feedback.
- The other players are still active, still practicing skills, and unable to hear your discussion.
- Because the rest of the team is still playing, you'll feel compelled to make your comments simple and concise—which, as we've said, is more helpful to the player.

This doesn't mean you can't use the team setting to give specific, positive feedback. You can do so to emphasize correct group and individual performances. Use this team feedback approach *only* for positive statements, though. Keep any negative feedback for individual discussions.

Developing Practice Plans

You will need to create practice plans for each season. Each practice plan should contain the following sections:

- Purpose
- Equipment
- Plan

Purpose sections focus on what you want to teach your players during each practice; they outline your main theme for each practice. The purpose should be drawn from your season plan (see chapter 9). Equipment sections note what you'll need to have on hand for that practice. Plan sections outline what you will do during each practice session. Each consists of these elements:

- Warm-Up
- Game
- Skill Practices
- Game
- Cool-Down and Wrap-Up

You'll begin each session with about five minutes of warm-up activities. Then you'll have your players play a modified football game (look in chapter 8 for suggested games and chapter 9 for their use in season plans). You'll look for your cue to interrupt that game—your cue being when players are having problems with carrying out the basic goal or aim of the game. At this point you'll "freeze" the action, keeping the players where they are, and ask brief questions about the tactical problems the players encountered and what skills they need to solve those problems. (Review chapter 4 for more on interrupting a game and holding a question-and-answer session.)

Then you'll teach the skill the players need to acquire to successfully execute the tactic. During Skill Practice you'll use the IDEA approach:

- Introduce the skill.
- Demonstrate the skill.
- Explain the skill.
- Attend to players practicing the skill.

Your introduction, demonstration, and explanation of a skill should take no more than two to three minutes; then you'll attend to players and provide teaching cues or further demonstration as necessary as they practice the skill.

After the Skill Practices, you will usually have the athletes play another game or two to let them use the skills they have just learned and to understand them in the context of a game. During Game and Skill Practices, emphasize the importance of every player on the field moving and being involved in every play, whether they will be directly touching the ball or not. No player on the field should be standing around.

The Plan section continues with a cool down and stretch. Following this you'll wrap up the practice with a few summary comments and remind them of the next practice or game day.

The games in chapter 8 include suggestions to help you modify the games. These suggestions will help you keep practices fun and provide activities for players with varying skill levels.

Although practicing using the games approach should reduce the need for discipline, there will be times when you'll have to deal with players who are misbehaving in practice. In the next section we'll help you handle these situations.

Dealing With Misbehavior

Athletes will misbehave at times; it's only natural. Following are two ways you can respond to misbehavior: through extinction or discipline.

Extinction

Ignoring a misbehavior—neither rewarding nor disciplining it—is called *extinction*. This can be effective under certain circumstances. In some situations, disciplining young people's misbehavior only encourages them to act up further because of the recognition they get. Ignoring misbehavior teaches youngsters that it is not worth your attention.

Sometimes, though, you cannot wait for a behavior to fizzle out. When players cause danger to themselves or others or disrupt the activities of others, you need to take immediate action. Tell the offending player that the behavior must stop and that discipline will follow if it doesn't. If the athlete doesn't stop misbehaving after the warning, discipline.

Extinction also doesn't work well when a misbehavior is self-rewarding. For example, you may be able to keep from grimacing if a youngster kicks you in the shin, but he still knows you were hurt. Therein lies the reward. In these circumstances, it is also necessary to discipline the player for the undesirable behavior.

Extinction works best in situations in which players are seeking recognition through mischievous behaviors, clowning, or grandstanding. Usually, if you are patient, their failure to get your attention will cause the behavior to disappear.

However, be alert that you don't extinguish desirable behavior. When youngsters do something well, they expect to be positively reinforced. Not rewarding them will likely cause them to discontinue the desired behavior.

Discipline

Some educators say we should never discipline young people, but should only reinforce their positive behaviors. They argue that discipline does not work, that it creates hostility and sometimes develops avoidance behaviors that may be more unwholesome than the original problem behavior. It is true that discipline does not always work and that it can create problems when used ineffectively, but when used appropriately, discipline is effective in eliminating undesirable behaviors without creating other undesirable consequences. You must use discipline effectively, because it is impossible to guide athletes through positive reinforcement and extinction alone. Discipline is part of the positive approach when these guidelines are followed:

- Discipline in a corrective way to help athletes improve now and in the future. Don't discipline to retaliate and make yourself feel better.

- Impose discipline in an impersonal way when athletes break team rules or otherwise misbehave. Shouting at or scolding athletes indicates that your attitude is one of revenge.

- Once a good rule has been agreed upon, ensure that athletes who violate it experience the unpleasant consequences of their misbehavior. Don't wave discipline threateningly over their heads. Just do it, but warn an athlete once before disciplining.

- Be consistent in administering discipline.

- Don't discipline using consequences that may cause you guilt. If you can't think of an appropriate consequence right away, tell the player you will talk with him or her after you think about it. You might consider involving the player in designing a consequence.

- Once the discipline is completed, don't make athletes feel they are "in the doghouse." Make them feel that they're valued members of the team again.

- Make sure that what you think is discipline isn't perceived by the athlete as a positive reinforcement—for instance, keeping a player out of doing a certain drill or portion of the practice may be just what the athlete desired.

- Never discipline athletes for making errors when they are playing.

- Never use physical activity—running laps or doing push-ups—as discipline. To do so only causes athletes to resent physical activity, something we want them to learn to enjoy throughout their lives.

- Discipline sparingly. Constant discipline and criticism cause athletes to turn their interests elsewhere and to resent you as well.

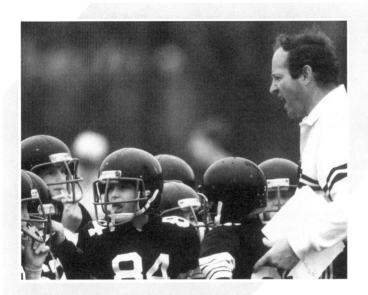

chapter 6

Game-Day Coaching

Contests provide the opportunity for your players to show what they've learned in practice. Just as your players' focus shifts on contest days from learning and practicing to *competing*, so your focus shifts from teaching skills to coaching players as they perform those skills in contests. Of course, the contest is a teaching opportunity as well, but the focus is on performing what has been previously learned.

In the last chapter you learned how to teach your players football tactics and skills; in this chapter we'll help you coach your players as they execute those tactics and skills in contests. We'll provide important coaching principles that will guide you throughout the game day—before, during, and after the contest.

Before the Contest

Just as you need a practice plan for what you're going to do each practice, you need a game plan for what to do on the day of a game. Many inexperienced coaches focus only on how they will coach during the contest itself, but your preparations to coach should include details that begin well before the first play of the game. In fact, your preparations should begin during the practice before the contest.

Preparations at Practice

During the practice a day or two before the next contest, you should do two things (besides practicing tactics and skills) to prepare your players: Decide on any specific team tactics that you want to employ, and discuss pregame particulars such as what to eat before the game, what to wear, and when to be at the field.

Deciding Team Tactics

Some coaches see themselves as great military strategists guiding their young warriors to victory on the battlefield. These coaches burn the midnight oil as they devise a complex plan of attack. There are several things wrong with this approach, but we'll point out two errors in terms of deciding team tactics:

1. The decision on team tactics should be made with input from players.
2. Team tactics at this level don't need to be complex.

Perhaps you guessed right on the second point but were surprised by the first. Why should you include your players in deciding tactics? Isn't that the coach's role?

It's the coach's role to help youngsters grow through the sport experience. Giving your athletes input here helps them to learn the game. It gets them involved at a planning level that often is reserved solely for the coach. It gives them a feeling of ownership; they're not just "carrying out orders" of the coach. They're executing the plan of attack that was jointly decided. Youngsters who have a say in how they approach a task often respond with more enthusiasm and motivation.

Don't dampen that enthusiasm and motivation by concocting tactics that are too complex. Keep tactics simple, especially at the younger levels. Focus on consistent execution, moving the ball on offense, and stopping long gains on defense.

As you become more familiar with your team's tendencies and abilities, help them focus on specific tactics that will help them play better. For example, if your team has a tendency to stand around and watch the action, emphasize the importance of teamwork and the responsibility of every player fulfilling his or her role. If they are active and moving throughout the game, but not in any cohesive fashion, focus them on knowing their assignments on offensive plays and defensive alignments.

Discussing Precontest Particulars

Players need to know what to do before a contest: what they should eat on game day and when, what clothing they should wear to the game, what equipment they should bring, and what time they should arrive at the field. Discuss these particulars with them at the practice before a contest. Here are guidelines for discussing these issues.

Pregame Meal. Carbohydrates are easily digested and absorbed and are a ready source of fuel. Players should eat a high-carbohydrate meal ideally about three to four hours before a game to allow the stomach to empty completely. This won't be possible for games held in early morning; in this case, athletes should still eat food high in carbohydrates, such as an English muffin, toast, or cereal, but not so much that their stomachs are full. In addition, athletes' pregame meals shouldn't include foods that are spicy or high in fat content.

Clothing and Equipment. Instruct players to wear their team uniforms, helmets, mouthguards, shoulder pads, girdle pads, thigh pads, knee pads, and shoes. If you are playing touch or flag football, they should wear T-shirts or jerseys; flags; shorts, football pants, or sweatpants; mouthguards; and tennis shoes or shoes with plastic cleats.

Time to Arrive. Your players will need to adequately warm up before a game, so instruct them to arrive 20 minutes before a game to go through a team warm-up (see "The Warm-Up" later in this chapter).

Facilities, Equipment, and Support Personnel

Although the site coordinator and officials have responsibilities regarding facilities and equipment, it's wise for you to know what to look for to make sure the contest is safe for the athletes. You should arrive at the field 25 to 30 minutes before game time so you can check the field, check in with the site coordinator and officials, and greet your players as they arrive to warm up. The site coordinator and officials should be checking the facilities and preparing for the contest. If officials aren't arriving before the game when they're supposed to, inform the site coordinator. A facilities checklist includes the following:

Field surface

- ✓ Sprinkler heads and openings are at grass level.
- ✓ The field is free of toxic substances (lime, fertilizer, and so on).

✔ The field is free of low spots or ruts.

✔ The playing surface is free of debris.

✔ No rocks or cement slabs are on the field.

✔ The field is free of protruding pipes, wires, and lines.

✔ The field is not too wet.

✔ The field is not too dry.

✔ The field lines are well marked.

Outside playing area

✔ The edge of the playing field is at least six feet from trees, walls, fences, and cars.

✔ Nearby buildings are protected (by fences, walls) from possible damage during play.

✔ Storage sheds and facilities are locked.

✔ The playground area (ground surface and equipment) is in safe condition.

✔ The fences/walls lining the area are in good repair.

✔ Sidewalks are without cracks, separations, or raised concrete.

Equipment

✔ Goals are held securely together.

Unplanned Events

Part of being prepared to coach is to expect the unexpected. What do you do if players are late? What if *you* have an emergency and can't make the game or will be late? What if the contest is rained out or otherwise postponed? Being prepared to handle out-of-the-ordinary circumstances will help you when such unplanned events happen.

If players are late, you may have to adjust your starting lineup. While this may not be a major inconvenience, do stress to your players the importance of being on time for two reasons:

⊙ Part of being a member of a team means being committed and responsible to the other members. When players don't show up, or show up late, they break that commitment.

⊙ Players need to go through a warm-up to physically prepare for the contest. Skipping the warm-up risks injury.

Communicating With Parents

The groundwork for your communication with parents will have been laid in the parent orientation meeting, through which parents learn the best ways to support their kids'—and the whole team's—efforts on the field. As parents gather at the field before a contest, let them know what the team has been focusing on during the past week and what your goals are for the game. For instance, perhaps you've worked on a pressure defense in practice this week; encourage parents to watch for improvement and success in the defense putting pressure on the offense and to support the players as they attempt all tactics and skills. Help parents to judge success not just based on the contest outcome, but on how the kids are improving their performances.

If parents yell at the kids for mistakes made during the game, make disparaging remarks about the officials or opponents, or shout instructions on what tactics to employ, ask them to refrain from making such remarks and to instead be supportive of the team in their comments and actions.

After a contest, briefly and informally assess with parents, as the opportunity arises, how the team did based not on the outcome, but on meeting performance goals and playing to the best of their abilities. Help parents see the contest as a process, not solely as a test that's pass/fail or win/lose. Encourage parents to reinforce that concept at home.

Consider making a team rule stating that players need to show up 20 minutes before a game and go through the complete team warm-up, or they won't start.

An emergency might cause *you* to be late or miss a game. In such cases, notify your assistant coach, if you have one, or the league coordinator. If notified in advance, a parent of a player or another volunteer might be able to step in for the contest.

Sometimes a game will be postponed because of inclement weather or for other reasons (such as unsafe field conditions). If the postponement takes place before game day, you'll need to call each member of your team to let him or her know. If it happens while the teams are on the field preparing for the game, gather your team members and tell them the news and why the game is being postponed. Make sure all your players have rides home before you leave—be the last to leave to be sure.

The Warm-Up

Players need to both physically and mentally prepare for a game once they arrive at the field. Physical preparation involves warming up. We've suggested that players arrive 20 minutes before the game to warm up. Conduct the warm-up similar to practice warm-ups, with some brief games that focus on skill practice and stretching.

Players should prepare to do what they will do in the game: block, run or pass the football, receive the ball, kick the ball, tackle, and cover receivers. This doesn't mean they spend extensive time on each skill; you can plan two or three brief practice games that encompass all these skills.

After playing a few brief games, your players should stretch. You don't need to deliver any big pep talk, but you can help your players mentally prepare as they stretch by reminding them of the following:

- The tactics and skills they've been working on in recent practices, especially focusing their attention on what they've been doing well. Focus on their strengths.
- The team tactics you decided on in your previous practice.
- Performing the tactics and skills to the best of their individual abilities and playing together as a team.
- Playing hard and smart and having fun!

During the Contest

The list you just read goes a long way toward defining your focus for coaching during the contest. Throughout the game, you'll keep the game in proper perspective and help your players do the same. You'll observe how your players execute tactics and skills and how well they play together. You'll make tactical decisions in a number of areas. You'll model appropriate behavior on the sideline, showing respect for opponents and officials, and demand the same of your athletes. You'll watch out for your athletes' physical safety and psychological welfare, in terms of building their self-esteem and helping them manage stress and anxiety.

Proper Perspective

Winning games is the short-term goal of your football program; helping your players learn the tactics, skills, and rules of football, how to become fit, and how to be good sports in football and in life is the long-term goal. Your young athletes are "winning" when they are becoming better human beings through their participation in football. Keep that perspective in mind when you coach. *You* have the privilege of setting the tone for how your team approaches the game. Keep winning and all aspects of the competition in proper perspective, and your young charges will likely follow suit.

Tactical Decisions

While you aren't called upon to be a great military strategist, you are called upon to make tactical decisions in several areas throughout a contest. You'll make decisions about who starts the game and when to enter substitutes; about making slight adjustments to your team's tactics; and about correcting players' performance errors or leaving the correction for the next practice.

Starting and Substituting Players

In considering playing time, make sure that everyone on the team gets to play at least half of each game. This should be your guiding principle as you consider starting and substitution patterns. We suggest you consider two options in substituting players:

○ **Substituting Individually.** Replace one player with another. This offers you a lot of latitude in deciding who goes in when, and it gives you the greatest mix of players throughout the game, but it can be hard to keep track of playing time (this could be made easier by assigning an assistant or a parent to this task). Remember that each player is required to play one half of each game.

○ **Substituting by Quarters.** The advantage here is that you can easily track playing time, and players know how long they will be in before they might be replaced.

Adjusting Team Tactics

At the 8 to 9 and 10 to 11 age levels, you probably won't adjust your team tactics too significantly during a game; rather, you'll focus on the basic tactics in general and emphasize during breaks which tactics your team needs to work on in particular. However, coaches of 12- to 14-year-olds might have cause to make tactical adjustments to improve their team's chances of performing well and winning. As games progress, assess your opponents' style of play and tactics, and make adjustments that are appropriate—that is, that your players are prepared for. Consider the following examples:

- Do your opponents have slow or lesser-skilled defensive backs? If so, you might want to emphasize your passing game.
- Do your opponents have skilled running backs that are threats to break open long runs? You might want to shift your defensive alignment to put more players on the line.
- Do your opponents always run on first down? Then stack the line against them on first downs.
- Does the opposing quarterback tend to make poor decisions and rush passes while under pressure? Then put more of a rush on him to try to create turnovers.

Knowing the answers to such questions can help you both formulate a game plan and make adjustments during a game. However, don't stress tactics *too* much during a game. Doing so can take the fun out of the game for the players. If you don't trust your memory, carry a pen and notepad to note which team tactics and individual skills need attention in the next practice.

Correcting Players' Errors

In chapter 5 you learned about two types of errors: learning errors and performance errors. Learning errors are ones that occur because athletes don't know how to perform a skill. Athletes make performance errors not because they don't know how to do the skill, but because they make a mistake in executing what they do know.

Sometimes it's not easy to tell which type of error athletes are making. Knowing your athletes' capabilities helps you to know whether they know the skill and are simply making mistakes in executing it or whether they don't really know how to perform the skill. If they are making learning errors—that is, they don't know how to perform the skills—you'll need to make note of this and teach them at the next practice. Game time is not the time to teach skills.

If they are making performance errors, however, you can help players correct those errors during a game. Players who make performance errors often do so because they have a lapse in concentration or motivation—or they are simply demonstrating the human quality of sometimes doing things incorrectly. A word of encouragement to concentrate more may help. If you do correct a performance error during a contest, do so in a quiet, controlled, and positive tone of voice during a break or when the player is on the sidelines with you.

For those making performance errors, you have to decide if it is just the occasional error anyone makes or an expected error for a youngster at that stage of development. If that is the case, then the player may appreciate your not commenting on the mistake. The player knows it was a mistake and knows how to correct it. On the other hand, perhaps an encouraging word and a "coaching cue" (such as "Remember to follow through on your passes") may be just what the athlete needs. Knowing the players and what to say is very much a part of the "art" of coaching.

Coach's and Players' Behavior

Another aspect of coaching on game day is managing behavior—both yours and your athletes'. The two are closely connected.

Your Conduct

You very much influence your players' behavior before, during, and after a contest. If you're up, your players are more likely to be up. If you're anxious, they'll notice and the anxiety can be contagious. If you're negative, they'll respond with worry. If you're positive, they'll play with more enjoyment. If you're constantly yelling instructions or commenting on mistakes and errors, it will be difficult for players to concentrate. Instead, let players get into the flow of the game.

The focus should be on positive competition and on having fun. A coach who overorganizes everything and dominates a game from the sideline is definitely *not* making the contest fun.

So how should you conduct yourself on the sideline? Here are a few pointers:

- Be calm, in control, and supportive of your players.
- Encourage players often, but instruct during play sparingly. Players should be focusing on their performance during a game, not on instructions shouted from the sidelines.
- If you need to instruct a player, do so when you're both on the sidelines, in an unobtrusive manner. Never yell at players for making a mistake. Instead, briefly demonstrate or remind them of the correct technique and encourage them.

Remember, you're not playing in the Super Bowl! In this program, football competitions are designed to help players develop their skills and themselves—and to have fun. So coach in a manner at games that helps your players do those things.

Players' Conduct

You're responsible for keeping your players under control. Do so by setting a good example and by disciplining when necessary. Set team rules of good behavior. If players attempt to cheat, fight, argue, badger, yell disparaging remarks, and the like, it is your responsibility to correct the misbehavior. Consider team rules in these areas of game conduct:

- Players' language
- Players' behavior
- Interactions with officials
- Discipline for misbehavior
- Dress code for competitions

Players' Physical Safety

We devoted all of chapter 3 to discussing how to provide for players' safety, but it's worth noting here that safety during contests can be affected by how officials are calling the rules. If they aren't calling rules correctly, and this risks injury to your players, you must intervene. Voice your concern in a respectful manner and in a way that places the emphasis where it should be: on the athletes' safety. One of the officials' main responsibilities is to provide for athletes' safety; you are not adversaries here. Don't hesitate to address an issue of safety with an official when the need arises.

Players' Psychological Welfare

Athletes often attach their self-worth to winning and losing. This idea is fueled by coaches, parents, peers, and society, who place great emphasis on winning. Players become anxious when they're uncertain if they can meet the expectations of others or of themselves when meeting these expectations is important to them.

   If you place too much importance on the game or cause your athletes to doubt their abilities, they will become anxious about the outcome and their performance. If your players look uptight and anxious during a contest, find ways to reduce both the uncertainties about how their performance will be evaluated and the importance they are attaching to the game. Help athletes focus on realistic personal goals—goals that are reachable and measurable and that will help them improve their performance. Another way to reduce anxiety on game day is to stay away from emotional pregame pep talks. We provided guidance earlier in what to address before the game.

   When coaching during contests, remember that the most important outcome from playing football is to build or enhance players' self-worth.

Keep that firmly in mind, and strive to make every coaching decision promote your athletes' self-worth.

Opponents and Officials

Respect opponents and officials. Without them, you wouldn't have a competition. Officials help provide a fair and safe experience for athletes and, as appropriate, help them learn the game. Opponents provide opportunities for your team to test itself, improve, and excel.

You and your team should show respect for opponents by giving your best efforts. You owe them this. Showing respect doesn't necessarily mean being "nice" to your opponents, though it does mean being civil.

Don't allow your players to "trash talk" or taunt an opponent. Such behavior is disrespectful to the spirit of the competition and to the opponent. Immediately remove a player from a contest if he disobeys your orders in this area.

Remember that officials are quite often teenagers—in many cases not much older than the players themselves. The level of officiating should be commensurate to the level of play. In other words, don't expect perfection from officials any more than you do from your own players. Especially at younger levels, they *won't* make every call, because to do so would stop the contest every 10 seconds.

After the Contest

When the game is over, join your team in congratulating the coaches and players of the opposing team, then be sure to thank the officials. Check on any injuries players sustained and let players know how to care for them. Be prepared to speak with the officials about any problems that occurred during the game. Then hold a brief Team Circle, as explained in a moment, to ensure your players are on an even keel, whether they won or lost.

Winning With Class, Losing With Dignity

When celebrating a victory, make sure your team does so in a way that doesn't show disrespect for the opponents. It's fine and appropriate to be happy and celebrate a win, but don't allow your players to taunt the opponents or boast about their victory. Keep winning in perspective. Winning and losing are a part of life, not just a part of sport. If players can handle both equally well, they'll be successful in whatever they do.

Athletes are competitors, and competitors will be disappointed in defeat. If your team has made a winning effort, let them know that. After a loss, help them keep their chins up and maintain a positive attitude that will carry over into the next practice and contest.

Team Circle

If your players have performed well in a game, compliment them and congratulate them immediately afterward. Tell them specifically what they did well, whether they won or lost. This will reinforce their desire to repeat their good performances.

Don't criticize individual players for poor performances in front of teammates. Help players improve their skills, but do so in the next practice, not immediately after a game.

The postgame Team Circle isn't the time to go over tactical problems and adjustments. The players are either so happy after a win or so dejected after a loss that they won't absorb much tactical information immediately following a game. Your first concern should be your players' attitudes and mental well-being. You don't want them to be too high after a win or too low after a loss. This is the time you can be most influential in keeping the outcome in perspective and keeping them on an even keel.

Finally, make sure your players have transportation home. Be the last one to leave in order to help if transportation falls through and to ensure full supervision of players before they leave.

chapter 7

Rules and Equipment

This is where we'll introduce you to some of the basic rules of football, both tackle football and flag and touch football. We won't try to cover all the rules of the game but rather will give you what you need to work with players who are 8 to 14 years old. We'll give you information on terminology, field size and markings, ball size, and equipment. Next we'll discuss player positions for both tackle football and flag and touch football. We'll then describe game procedures and scoring, and follow that with the rules of play. Finally, we'll talk about officiating and show you some of the officiating signals for football.

Terms to Know

Tackle football and flag and touch football have their own vocabularies. Being familiar with common terms will make your job easier.

Tackle Football

audible—Using a vocal signal at the line of scrimmage to change the play previously called in the huddle.

backfield—Players who are one yard or more behind the scrimmage line when the ball is snapped.

blitz—When a defense commits extra players, in addition to linemen, to rush the passer.

chains—Ten-yard length of chain used to measure distance required for a first down.

cross block—Two linemen blocking defenders who are diagonally opposite the blockers' own starting positions; one of the blockers moves first.

defensive formation—An alignment of defensive linemen, linebackers, and defensive backs positioned to stop a particular offense.

downs—A series of four consecutive charged scrimmages allotted to the offensive team; to retain possession the offense must advance the ball to a yard line called the necessary line during these scrimmages.

eligible receiver—Any offensive player who is legally in the backfield or any player on either end of the line of scrimmage.

end zone—That area bounded by the goal line, end line, and sidelines.

fair catch—The unhindered catch by a member of the receiving team of any kick that has crossed the kicking team's line of scrimmage or free-kick line, provided the proper signal (that is, one hand and arm extended above the head and moving them side to side) has been given by the receiver.

field goal—A placekick or dropkick from scrimmage that goes through the uprights of the goal without touching the ground first. Three points are awarded for a field goal.

first down—The first of four allotted downs the offensive team receives, occurring when the offensive team gains 10 or more yards within its allotted four downs.

forward pass—A pass that strikes anything beyond the spot from which the pass is thrown; a pass in the direction of the opponents' goal.

fumble—A player's losing possession of the football other than by passing or kicking it.

goal line defense—Defensive alignment used near the defensive team's own goal line that places defensive linemen in the six gaps and has all defensive players close to the line of scrimmage in an attempt to stop the anticipated running play.

goal post—A structure placed on each end line of the field; attempts at field goals and extra points must pass through the goal posts to be successful.

handoff—The ball being handed (not passed or lateraled) from one player to another. The quarterback usually executes a handoff to a running back, but a running back might also execute a handoff to the receiver on a reverse.

hash mark—Line running the length of the field bisecting the yard lines. The ball is not placed outside the hash marks when a play is to begin.

I formation—Offensive formation in which a fullback and tailback are positioned in a line directly behind the quarterback—the center, quarterback, fullback, and tailback form an "I."

illegal use of hands—With possession of the ball established by either team, a player's using the hands to grasp and impede an opponent who is not a ball carrier.

ineligible receiver—A player on the line of scrimmage (with at least one other player on either side of him) who cannot legally catch a pass or—on a pass play—be downfield before a pass is thrown.

interception—Gaining possession of the ball; occurs when a defender catches a pass thrown by the offense.

kickoff—A free kick initiating each half of play; it also follows the scoring of a field goal or extra point. The ball is either placed on the kicking team's 40-yard line on a kicking tee or held by a player on the kicking team. All players on the kicking team must remain behind their 40-yard line until the ball is kicked. Once the ball travels 10 yards downfield, either team can establish position.

kickoff return—The team receiving a kickoff establishes possession of the ball and attempts to advance the ball upfield.

late hit—An infraction occurring when a player hits an opponent after the whistle has already blown the play dead.

lateral pass—When the ball is tossed or thrown backward. (If it is dropped, it is considered a fumble.)

line of scrimmage—An imaginary line running perpendicular to the sidelines. The offensive and defensive lines of scrimmage are located on either end of the neutral zone and mark the ball's position at the start of each down.

man-to-man coverage—Defensive pass coverage in which defenders are assigned specific receivers to cover; they cover those receivers no matter where they run their routes.

neutral zone—Area located within the width of the football.

offensive formation—The offensive team's lineup; that is, the locations of the offensive players before the snap of the ball.

onside kick—A play in which a kickoff is deliberately made short, so that the team kicking off has a chance to get possession of the ball.

option—An offensive play designed to give the ball carrier the opportunity to carry the ball upfield, hand the ball off, or pass it to a teammate.

passing route—The path a receiver takes in an attempt to get open to receive a pass (or to serve as a decoy).

pass rush—A defender's attempt to tackle or hurry a member of the offensive team attempting to pass the football.

placekick—A play in which the ball is kicked from a tee or from the hold of a member of the kicking team, used for field goals and kickoffs.

play-action pass—A play in which a fake handoff precedes a pass attempt—this kind of pass is designed to pull in the linebackers and defensive backs and to slow the pass rush (by making the defense think the play is a run).

possession—Having control of the ball.

punt—Kicking the ball after dropping it and before it reaches the ground. Offensive teams who have failed to cover 10 yards in their first three attempts often use a punt on the fourth down.

punt coverage—When a ball is punted, players of the punting team running downfield in an attempt to tackle an opponent who has fielded the punted ball and not called for a fair catch.

punt return—A player who has received a punted ball tries to advance it.

quarterback sneak—A quarterback running or diving over the line of scrimmage.

roughing the passer—An infraction that occurs when a defensive player hits the quarterback after the ball has been released. The official must decide whether the defensive player had time to stop after the ball's release.

sack—The action of a defender tackling the quarterback behind the line of scrimmage.

shotgun—An offensive formation in which the quarterback is lined up in the backfield about 5 to 7 yards behind the center.

snap—The quick exchange of the football from the center to the quarterback to put the ball into play.

T formation—An offensive formation in which the fullback is positioned 2 to 4 yards behind a quarterback who is positioned immediately behind the center. One halfback is on either side of the fullback, and the fullback and the two halfbacks are in a line parallel with the line of scrimmage.

time-out—The clock's being stopped at the request of a player of either team. In general, each team is allowed three such requests during each half of a game.

touchback—Balls kicked through the end zone or downed in the receiving team's end zone. The referee then places the ball on the receiving team's 20-yard line for it to start from.

trap block—Technique in which an offensive lineman pulls out of the line and blocks an unsuspecting defender elsewhere down the line.

two-point conversion—Successfully running or passing the ball into the end zone from the 3-yard line following a touchdown.

wishbone—An offensive formation in which the quarterback is under center (direct snap), a fullback is directly behind the quarterback, and two halfbacks are behind and to the sides of the fullback.

zone coverage—Defensive pass coverage in which defenders are assigned specific areas to cover and cover anyone coming into these areas.

Flag and Touch Football

contact blocking—Open-hand, straight-arm blocking between two players. Contact above the shoulders or below the waist is not permitted. Players may not leave their feet to block.

deflagging—The legal removal of a flag from an opponent in possession of the ball. Pushing, striking, holding, slapping, or tripping when attempting to pull a flag is not permitted. Defensive players may leave their feet to pull a flag. Offensive players are not permitted to protect or guard their flags.

flag removal—When the flag is clearly taken from the runner, the down is over and the ball is declared dead. A player who removes the flag from the runner should immediately hold the flag above her head to assist the official in locating the spot where the capture occurred. If a flag inadvertently falls to the ground, a two-hand tag between the shoulders and knees constitutes capture.

fumble—There are no fumbles in flag and touch football. Once the ball hits the ground during a play, it is ruled dead at the spot.

protected scrimmage kick—A punt. The punting team may request that the defense not rush until the ball is punted.

screen blocking—A form of blocking with no contact between players. The player's arms must be at his side when making a screen block. Players may not leave their feet to screen block.

touching—Simultaneous placing of both hands anywhere between the shoulders and knees of an opponent who has the ball. This includes the ball in the ball carrier's possession. The feet of the toucher may leave the ground to make a touch. Pushing, striking, slapping, and holding are not permitted. Tripping the ball carrier in an attempt to make a diving tag results in a penalty.

zone line to gain—The next line on the playing field in the direction of, and parallel to, the opponent's goal line. The down box is stationed at the zone line to gain.

Field

Most youth programs follow Pop Warner Football's guidelines for fields, with 80 yards between goal lines and 40 yards between sidelines (see figure 7.1). Some programs start players on even smaller 60-by-30-yard fields.

In flag and touch football, your field is broken into stationary 20-yard zones with first downs being achieved by crossing the next zone line to gain (see figure 7.2). For example, it can be first down and 2 yards to go or first down and 19 yards to go, with the first down reached at the next zone line to gain! Field dimensions can be altered to fit your needs or constraints of space (see figure 7.3, a-b).

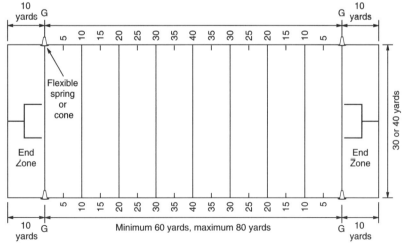

Figure 7.1   Regulation tackle football field.

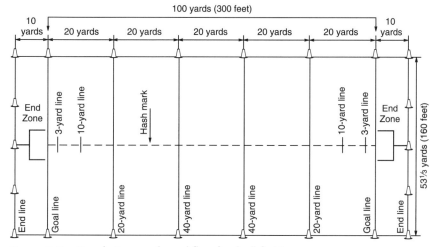

Figure 7.2   Regulation touch and flag football field.

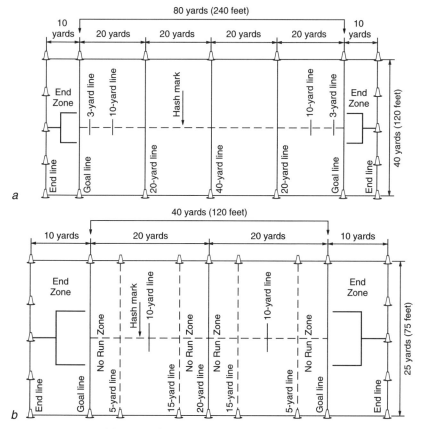

Figure 7.3   (a) Abbreviated touch and flag football field. (b) 4 v 4 touch and flag football field.

Ball

Just as the size of the field is reduced to match players' development, so too is the size of the ball (see tables 7.1 and 7.2). Your league will probably distribute to all teams a certain size and brand of ball to use throughout the season. The ball will have a set of laces and a leather, rubber, or plastic surface. Check the air pressure of the inflated rubber bladder inside to make sure it agrees with the pressure amount designated on the ball's exterior.

Table 7.1   Pop Warner Football Designated Age-Group Divisions and Ball Dimensions

Age group	Division	Football dimensions (inches)
7-9	Mighty Mites	$10\frac{1}{4}$ to $10\frac{1}{2}$
8-10	Junior Pee Wees	
9-11	Pee Wees	
10-12	Junior Midgets	$10\frac{5}{8}$ to $10\frac{3}{4}$
11-13	Midgets	
12-14	Junior Bantams	
14	Bantams	11 to $11\frac{1}{2}$ (regulation)

Table 7.2   USFTL Designated Age-Group Divisions and Ball Dimensions

Age group	Football dimensions
6 and under	In flag and touch football, the quarterback may choose the size of ball he will use. If he has a large hand, he may choose to use a regulation-size ball. If he has a small hand, he may use a smaller ball (youth, junior, or intermediate).
8 and under	
10 and under	
12 and under	
14 and under	
16 and under	
18 and under	

Any junior or youth size ball is allowed. The smaller size lets a younger player learn the proper techniques of throwing or carrying a football at an earlier age.

Player Equipment

The physical nature of tackle football requires that players wear protective gear. These items include a helmet, mouthguard, shoulder pads, girdle pads, thigh pads, knee pads, and shoes.

Examine the condition of each item you distribute to players. Also check that the pieces of equipment they furnish for themselves meet acceptable standards. In addition, it is important that each piece of equipment is fit to the player. Check that each athlete on your team is outfitted properly. That means following the guidelines in figure 7.4 for

Shoulder pads	Body padding should not extend beyond tip of shoulder; neck area should fit snugly when arms are extended over head.
Helmet	Must fit snugly around head and in jaw section; head should be in contact with crown suspension when front edge is approximately one inch above the eyebrow.
Clothing	Jersey should fit close to body and should always be tucked in pants to hold shoulder pad in place; pants should hug body to keep thigh and knee guards in place.
Mouthguard	Mouthguard should fit properly.
Girdle pads	Hip pads must cover the point of hip and give proper lower-spine protection.
Thigh and knee pads	Must be the proper size and inserted properly in the lining of the player's pants.
Shoes	Cleats should be inspected regularly to ensure even wear and stability; proper width is very important; upper should never "overrun" outsole.

Figure 7.4 Tackle football equipment.

fitting a tackle football uniform to a player and in figure 7.5 for fitting a flag or touch football uniform to a player.

You may have to demonstrate to players how to put on each piece of equipment. Otherwise, expect some of them to show up for the first practice with their shoulder pads on backward and their thigh pads upside down.

Shaping a mouthguard is also a mystery to most youngsters. Although these plastic mouthpieces come with easy-to-follow directions, your players may need further guidance. Take some time to explain the heating and shaping process.

The helmet is the most commonly misused piece of football equipment. So before distributing helmets to your players, explain very clearly that a helmet is a protective covering, not a weapon. If you spot a player using the helmet as a battering device, take him aside and demonstrate the correct, heads-up technique.

T-shirt or jersey	Should be tucked in so hands are not injured reaching for flags.
Flags	Flag football only.
Shorts, football pants, or sweatpants	Pants should fit properly.
Socks	Socks should be clean and dry.
Shoes	Tennis shoes or spikes with plastic cleats only.
Mouthguard	Mouthguard should fit properly.

Figure 7.5 Touch and flag football equipment.

Player Positions

Give your young athletes a chance to play a variety of positions, on both offense and defense. By playing different positions, they'll become better all-around players and will probably stay more interested in the sport. Furthermore, they'll have a better understanding of the many skills and tactics used in the game. They will also better appreciate the efforts of their teammates who play positions they find difficult.

Here are descriptions of the offensive, defensive, and special-teams positions for both tackle football and flag and touch football.

Offensive Positions in Tackle Football

Figure 7.6 illustrates a basic 11-player offensive alignment. Here's a brief outline of the desired attributes and responsibilities of players at each position.

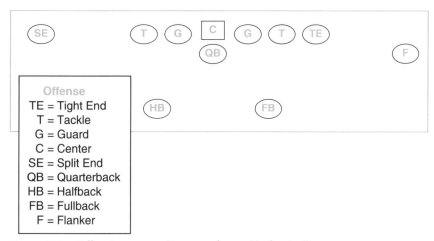

Offense
TE = Tight End
T = Tackle
G = Guard
C = Center
SE = Split End
QB = Quarterback
HB = Halfback
FB = Fullback
F = Flanker

Figure 7.6 Offensive team alignment for tackle football.

Offensive Linemen

Ideally, you'll be able to put big, strong, and quick athletes into the center, guard, and tackle positions. These players must block and open up holes for ball carriers to run through. When a pass play is called, they must protect the quarterback from opposing linemen.

Receivers

Another player who has important blocking duties is the tight end, positioned on the line of scrimmage, next to (within 3 yards of) either tackle. The tight end must be strong enough to block a defensive end, yet speedy enough to get open on pass routes.

The two other receiver positions are the flanker and the split end, or wide receiver. Speed and agility, along with great catching ability, are the qualities to look for in filling these spots. The flanker can be positioned on either side, off the line of scrimmage, whereas the split end is 8 to 10 yards outside the opposite tackle and up on the line. When the flanker is on the split end side, he is referred to as the slot.

Quarterback

Lined up directly behind the center to receive the snap, the quarterback is the field general of the offense. The quarterback calls the plays in the huddle, barks out the snap count at the line of scrimmage, and then, after taking the snap, hands the ball off, runs with it, or passes it.

At this position you'll want a good communicator and good athlete who can handle many responsibilities. To complete your wish list, the quarterback will have an excellent throwing arm.

Running Backs

Most teams use a two-back set, either a split-back formation like the one shown in figure 7.6 or an I formation in which the backs line up in a straight line behind the quarterback.

Often, one running back is called a fullback and the other a halfback. The fullback has more blocking responsibilities and is expected to pick up short yardage when needed. Therefore, you'll want a strong, fairly fast, and dependable player at this position. The halfback (called the tailback in the I formation) is the primary ball carrier. Speed and agility to outrun and outmaneuver would-be tacklers are desirable attributes for a halfback.

Some coaches prefer to line up their teams in a three-back set, moving the flanker to a wingback (WB) (see figure 7.7) in the single-wing formation or to a second halfback position to form a wishbone alignment (see figure 7.8). Coaches typically use the single-wing and wishbone formations when they want their teams to run the ball much more than pass it.

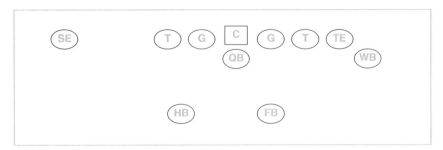

Figure 7.7 Single-wing formation.

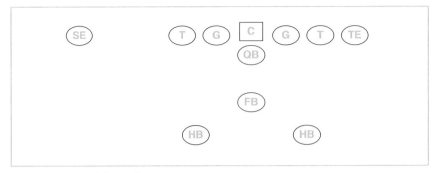

Figure 7.8 Wishbone formation.

Offensive Positions in Flag and Touch Football

Figure 7.9 illustrates a basic eight-player offensive alignment. In flag and touch football, all players are eligible receivers. Here's a brief outline of the desired attributes and responsibilities of players at each position.

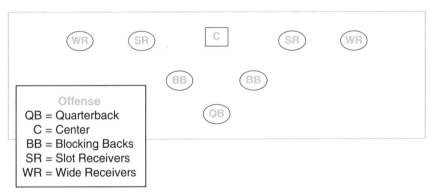

Offense
QB = Quarterback
C = Center
BB = Blocking Backs
SR = Slot Receivers
WR = Wide Receivers

Figure 7.9 Offensive team alignment for flag and touch football.

Quarterback

The quarterback lines up 5 to 7 yards behind the center in the offensive backfield, in what is sometimes called the shotgun formation. He should have the same attributes as a quarterback in tackle football.

Center

The center lines up on the line of scrimmage and is an eligible pass receiver in flag and touch football. She must be able to snap the ball back to the quarterback in a shotgun formation with speed and accuracy.

Blocking Backs

The blocking backs are eligible pass receivers, lined up in the offensive back field about 3 to 5 yards from the line of scrimmage. Their job is to protect the quarterback and receive passes. They also may be split out to "flood" a side of the field with several receivers.

Slot Receivers

The slot receivers take positions halfway between the center and the wide receivers. They must be fast and agile with good receiving abilities.

Wide Receivers

The wide receivers take positions on the outside ends of the line of scrimmage. They are usually the team's fastest players who can also run good patterns and have good hands.

The spread formation (see figure 7.10) is used to spread a defense and make it possible for the quarterback to find a "hot," or wide-open, receiver.

The triple-wing formation (see figure 7.11) is used when a team has more than one good quarterback. This formation creates a wide-open style of offense by making the defense uncertain about who will throw the ball.

Figure 7.10　Spread formation for flag and touch football.

Figure 7.11　Triple-wing formation for flag and touch football.

Defensive Positions in Tackle Football

Now it's time to look at the players you'll be asking to stop the opposing team from moving the football. Here are the basic defensive positions, with a short discussion of the skills and duties of each one.

Defensive Linemen

Youth football coaches put four to six players up front, on the line. The four-man front consists of two tackles and two ends. The five-man front adds a nose guard in the middle; the six-man front adds two ends who start in an upright position, much like outside linebackers (see next section).

Defensive tackles and defensive ends are primarily responsible for finding out who has the football and tackling him before he can gain yardage. It is also their duty to rush the passer when the offense attempts to throw the ball. To carry out their assignments, it is helpful for defensive linemen to have adequate size and strength as well as great quickness to fend off or avoid blocks by offensive players.

Linebackers

Depending on the number of linemen you use, you will want two to four linebackers on defense. No matter how many you use, each should have a nose for the ball—that is, he should be able to read the offense's play and stop it quickly.

The standard three-linebacker set shown in figure 7.12 complements the four-man front nicely. In this alignment, you have a middle linebacker at the heart of the defense and two outside linebackers.

The middle linebacker should be one of your best athletes and surest tacklers. The outside linebacker on the tight end side, often called Sam for short to indicate that he plays on the offense's strong side, must be strong enough to fend off blocks but also fast enough to cover the tight end on pass routes. Will, the weakside linebacker, must be able to stand his ground against blocks by linemen and backs to prevent the offense from running the ball successfully.

Defensive Backs

The players responsible for preventing long runs and completed passes by the offense are the defensive backs. Again, depending on the alignment of your defensive front, the offense's set, and the game situation, you'll have three to five defensive backs in the game. Safeties have run and pass responsibilities. Cornerbacks cover the wide-outs.

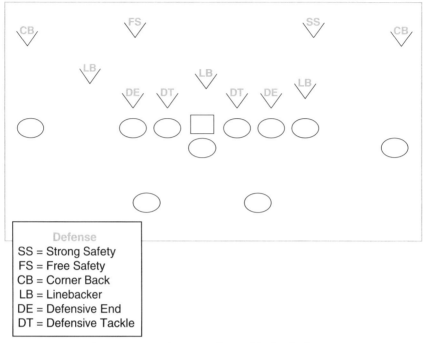

Figure 7.12   Defensive team alignment for tackle football.

All of these players must be agile and fast to cover speedy receivers. In addition, the safeties must be good tacklers to assist linebackers in stopping the run.

Defensive Positions in Flag and Touch Football

Here's a short discussion of the skills and duties of the basic defensive positions in flag and touch football (see figure 7.13).

Defensive End

The defensive ends are strong and quick players who rush the quarterback.

Nose Tackle

The nose tackle is a strong, quick player who rushes the quarterback and stops the run.

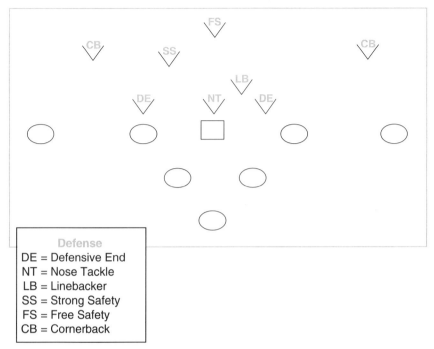

Figure 7.13   Defensive team alignment for flag and touch football.

Linebacker

Linebackers usually captain the defense and call defensive signals. They must be strong and quick with a keen sense of timing because they are in the middle of almost every play on defense.

Strong Safety

The strong safety is a defensive back who can double as a linebacker in certain defenses. He must be quick, agile, and strong enough to be able to cover and react to the ball.

Free Safety

The free safety is positioned at the deepest point of the defense. She is the last player between the defense and the goal line. She must be a very smart player because her primary responsibility is to read and go to the ball. She must also be fast.

Cornerback

The cornerbacks must be the fastest players on defense because it is their responsibility to cover the fastest players on offense, the wide receivers. They must be able to read and react, but they must also be able to come up in certain situations if the offense is trying a trick play, such as a double pass or an end around.

Special-Teams Positions for Tackle Football

Besides assigning players to the basic offensive and defensive spots, you'll need to designate players for special-teams positions. Here is a quick look at the key positions on each unit for tackle football.

Punt and Kick Teams

Long snapper: Center on field goal and punt teams

Holder: Player who receives snap on field goal attempts and places the ball on the tee for the kicker

Kicker: Kicker on kickoff, field goal, and PAT teams (see figure 7.14)

Punter: Kicker on punt team

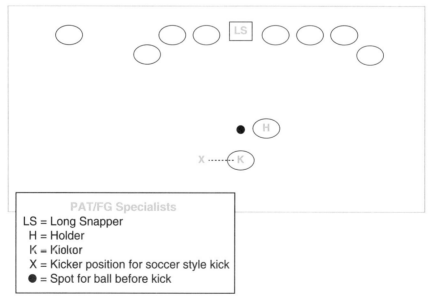

PAT/FG Specialists
LS = Long Snapper
H = Holder
K = Kicker
X = Kicker position for soccer style kick
● = Spot for ball before kick

Figure 7.14   Alignment for a PAT or field goal.

Punt and Kickoff Return Teams

Kick returner: Player farthest from kicker, whom the kickoff return team most wants to field and run with the ball

Punt returner: Player farthest from punter, whom the punt return team most wants to field and run with the ball

Special-Teams Positions for Flag and Touch Football

Here's a quick look at the key positions for flag and touch football special teams.

Punt Teams

Center: Player who snaps the ball back to the punter in a rapid and accurate motion

Punter: The kicker on the punt team

Linemen: Players who go down and pull the flag or touch the kick returner (see figure 7.15)

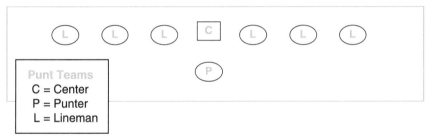

Figure 7.15   Punt team alignment for flag and touch football.

Kickoff Teams

Safety back: Player on a kickoff team responsible for stopping an opposing player who breaks a long return

Kicker: Kicker on kickoff teams

Linemen: Players who go down and pull the flag or touch the kick returner

Kickoff Return Teams

Kick returner: Player farthest from kicker, whom the kickoff return team most wants to field and run with the ball

Upback: Player who blocks for kick returner and sometimes returns short kick; field general of return teams who calls the directions of the returns

Linemen: Players who block for kick returns (see figure 7.16)

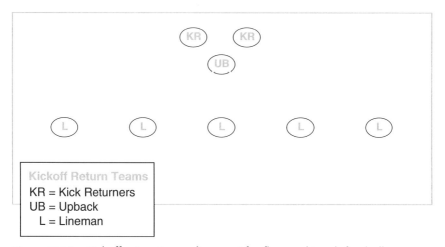

Figure 7.16   Kickoff return team alignment for flag and touch football.

Punt Return Teams

Punt returner: Player farthest from punter, whom the punt return team most wants to field and run with the ball

Upback: Player who blocks for punt returners, sometimes returns short punts; field general of return teams who calls the directions for the returners

Linemen: Players who block for punt returners

Extra Point and Field Goal Teams

Placekicker: Kicker on kickoff, field goal, and PAT teams

Holder: Player who receives snap on field goal attempts and places the ball on the tee for the kicker

Center: Player who snaps ball on field goal and extra point teams

Floater: Player who calls the plays on field goals and extra point attempts; lines up wherever she sees the most need, perhaps to help block on one side; may also call for a fake field goal or extra point

Guard: Player who blocks for kicker and holder; lines up next to center

Tackle: Player who blocks for kicker and holder; lines up next to guard on outside of line (see figure 7.17)

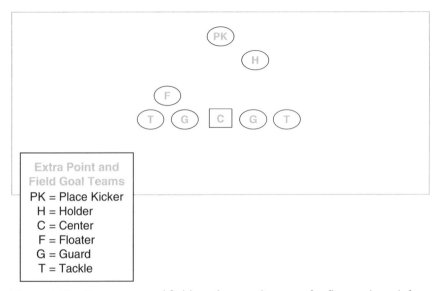

Figure 7.17 Extra point and field goal team alignment for flag and touch football.

How the Game Is Played

The game begins with a kickoff. A player on one team kicks the ball from a designated yard line off a tee toward the opponent's goal line. A player on either team can field the ball after it travels 10 yards downfield. If, as usually happens, a player on the receiving team gains possession, that player tries to advance the ball as far as possible toward the kicking team's goal line. The kicking team tries to tackle the ball carrier, pull the ball carrier's flag (in flag football), or touch the ball carrier (in touch football), as close to the receiving team's goal as possible. When any of these three things happen or the ball carrier runs out of bounds, the officials whistle the ball dead and momentarily stop play.

The point where play resumes is called the line of scrimmage. The line of scrimmage stretches from one sideline to the other, passing through the point of the ball nearest the defense. The team with the ball is the offense; the opposing team is the defense. In 11-man football, the offensive team must begin each play with at least 7 players lined up on the line of scrimmage, facing the defense. Each play starts when one of these linemen, the center, snaps the ball to a teammate, typically the quarterback.

The offense is allowed four plays, or downs, to advance the football 10 yards toward the opponent's goal line. If successful, the offense is given a new set of downs and can maintain possession until it

- is stopped by the defense and has to punt, typically on fourth down;
- turns the ball over to the defense by means of a fumble, interception, or failure to gain 10 yards in four attempts;
- attempts a field goal; or
- scores a touchdown.

In flag and touch football, a team achieves a first down by passing a stationary zone line to gain, located at the 20- and 40-yard lines.

Scoring

The primary objective of the offensive team is to score, although many coaches also want their offense to maintain possession of the ball for as long as possible. By doing so, they reduce the number of chances that the opposing team's offense has to score.

The defensive team's main objective is to prevent the offense from scoring. In addition, the defense tries to make the offensive team give up possession of the ball as far as possible from the goal line it is defending.

Offenses and defenses have many strategic options available to accomplish these objectives. Read chapter 8 for information on how to teach your team basic offensive and defensive tactics.

Rules of Play

Football rules are designed to make the game run smoothly and safely and prevent either team from gaining an unfair advantage. Throw out the rules, and a tackle football game quickly turns into a chaotic and dangerous competition where size, brute strength, and speed dominate.

Your league should already have rules concerning acceptable height and weight maximums and minimums for players. Even so, make sure your kids are matched up against opponents with similar physiques and skills. Discourage players from cutting weight to be eligible for your team. And, if you spot a mismatch during a game, talk with the opposing coach to see if you can cooperate and correct the problem.

Your league will also specify the length of your games. Typically, youth tackle football games consist of four 8- or 10-minute quarters. The clock is stopped when

- there is a change of possession,
- the ball goes out of bounds,
- an incomplete pass is thrown,
- the yard markers need to be advanced after a team gains 10 yards for a first down,
- a player is injured and officials call a time-out,
- a team scores, or
- a team calls a time-out.

You will be given two or three time-outs in each half. Use them wisely, not just for talking strategy. Remember, although the games may seem short to you, young players can easily become fatigued. So, besides substituting regularly, call a time-out when you see that your team is tired.

The time of games for flag and touch football is two 24-minute halves. The clock runs continuously for the first 22 minutes of each half and stops only for time-outs and scores. After the 2-minute warning, the clock stops for each event that it stops for in tackle football. Three time-outs per half are allowed, but you must use one of your time-outs before the 2-minute warning or you lose it.

Rule Infractions

The United States Flag and Touch Football League, Pop Warner Football, and your local youth football program have rule books available for your use. Take the time to study and learn the ins and outs, and then teach the rules to your football team.

Although no youth football team will perform penalty free, teach your players to avoid recurring penalties. By instilling this discipline, you'll help them enjoy more success, both as individuals and as a team.

Here is a brief list of common infractions that football players commit.

◉ **Offside:** Defensive player in or beyond the neutral zone when the ball is snapped

◉ **Encroachment:** Offensive player in or beyond the neutral zone before the ball is snapped

◉ **Illegal procedure:** Failure of the offensive team to have seven players on the line of scrimmage (in 11-man football); failure of offensive teams to have four players on the line of scrimmage at the snap (in 8-player flag and touch football); the offensive team having more than one player in motion or a player moving toward the line of scrimmage before the snap

◉ **Delay of game:** Offensive team taking more than 25 seconds to snap the ball after the referee has marked it ready for play

◉ **Holding:** Any player using the arms to hook or lock up an opponent to impede his movement; an offensive player extending the arms outside his body frame to grab an opponent

◉ **Pass interference (defensive):** Defensive player making contact with an eligible receiver who is beyond the neutral zone with the intent of impeding the offensive player trying to catch a catchable forward pass

As you teach your athletes to play with discipline and to avoid such rule violations, remember that you are their model. Players will reflect the discipline that you display in teaching them in practices and coaching them from the sidelines during games. So show respect for the rules, and don't shrug off game infractions or personal misconduct. And provide a great example by communicating respectfully with the individuals who officiate your games.

Playing by the Rules

You are in a position to teach your players more than simply obeying the rules of the game. As a coach, you have a responsibility to teach them only those techniques that are safe.

For example, in tackle football you must discourage spearing on defense, as it's against the rules. But it's also essential to teach young players never to lead with their heads when blocking or running. Kicking or striking an opponent or jumping on the pile at the conclusion of a play is not acceptable. Also, teach your players not to grasp an opponent's face mask because doing so can cause serious neck injuries.

If you fail to do so, you are directly contributing not only to the next penalty one of your players commits but also to the next injury one of your players suffers.

Tackle football is a contact, perhaps collision, sport. If participants play according to the letter and spirit of the rules, youngsters can participate safely. Make certain that your players do. The proper football techniques to teach young football players are described in chapter 8. "Tackle Football No-Nos" and "Flag and Touch Football No-Nos" list the techniques that you should not tolerate.

Tackle Football No-Nos

It's inevitable that your players will violate minor rules during practices and games; even pros go offside now and then. But make clear to your players that some actions are unacceptable on the football field. Officials typically call unsportsmanlike conduct penalties or personal fouls for these actions.

○ Tripping
○ Face masking (pulling on an opponent's face mask)
○ Blocking or tackling with a closed fist
○ Spearing (tackling with top of helmet)
○ Swearing
○ Taunting
○ Fighting
○ Clipping (blocking a player in the back)
○ Clotheslining (knocking a player down with a blow to the head or neck)

Flag and Touch Football No-Nos

- Illegally secured flag belt
- Spiking, kicking, throwing, or not returning the ball to the official during dead ball
- Hurdling
- Driving or running into a player
- Two-on-one blocking
- Tackling a runner
- Roughing the passer
- Illegal contact
- Tripping
- Swearing
- Taunting
- Fighting
- Clipping
- Contact with anything but open, extended arms

Promote good sportsmanship along with the use of proper fundamentals. Encourage players to help opponents up from the ground after a play. Ask ball carriers to hand the ball to the referee or leave it on the ground where they were stopped. The official will appreciate such behavior, and so will the players' parents, league administrators, and players' future coaches.

Officiating

Football rules are enforced by a crew of officials on the field. In youth tackle football, as many as seven officials or as few as two may work the games. Referees are the officials who control the game, marking the ball ready for play; signal penalties, time-outs, and first downs; and communicate with team captains and coaches. Figure 7.18 a-o shows common officiating signals.

If you have a concern about how a game is being officiated, address the referees respectfully. Do so immediately if at any time you feel that the officiating jeopardizes the safety of your players.

Figure 7.18 Officiating signal for: *(a)* time-out, *(b)* touchdown, field goal, *(c)* personal foul, *(d)* illegal use of hands, *(e)* illegal contact, *(f)* delay of game, *(g)* offside or encroaching, *(h)* holding, *(i)* illegal motion, *(j)* first down, *(k)* pass interference, *(l)* incomplete pass, penalty refused, missed kick, *(m)* failure to wear required equipment, *(n)* flag guarding, *(o)* roughing kicker or holder.

Figure 7.18 *(continued)*

90

chapter 8

Tactics and Skills

As your athletes play games in practice, their experience in these games—and your subsequent discussions with them about their experience—will lead them to the tactics and skills they need to develop to succeed. In the games approach, teaching tactics and teaching skills go hand in hand.

In this chapter we'll provide information for you to teach your players team tactics and individual offensive and defensive skills. Remember to use the IDEA approach to teaching skills—introduce, demonstrate, and explain the skill, and attend to players as they practice the skill. For a refresher on IDEA, see chapter 5.

This chapter ties directly to the season plans in chapter 9, describing the tactics and skills that you'll teach at practices. If you aren't familiar with football skills, rent or purchase a video to see the skills performed. You may also find advanced books on skills helpful.

We've only provided information about the basics of football in this book. As your players advance in their skills, you'll need to advance your knowledge as a coach. You can do so by learning from your experiences, watching and talking with more experienced coaches, and studying advanced resources.

Offensive Tactics

The objectives you set must be realistic and important—not just to you, but to your players. If your team is incapable of reaching the goals, or is not interested in achieving them, then they serve little purpose.

Scoring is the obvious objective when a team is on offense. But scoring is an outcome produced by the team's ability to

- execute consistently,
- move the football, and
- maintain possession.

To execute, move the ball, and maintain possession, you have to have a balanced attack, with both a strong passing game and a good running game, to keep the defense off balance. We'll look at aspects of the passing and running game—including the hurry-up offense and the run-and-shoot offense—after we explore the first three tactics. We'll also show you an offensive numbering system and a number of passing and running plays that can get you started.

Execute Consistently

To execute consistently, you must run the same plays throughout the season and work on them continually. Select a simple offense and teach it well. A few well-executed plays can give even the best opponents all they can handle. If your offense has too many plays, chances are your team members, not your opponents, will be confused.

Consistent execution stems from your athletes' understanding the plays and practicing them repeatedly. Every player must know what is expected of him or her for each play. Practicing these plays against the defense that you expect opponents to play will help your players visualize the way they should run each play. If your players know that a team goal is consistent execution, they'll be more eager to perform the plays as often as necessary to make them work in a game.

Teach your receivers the proper patterns to run and your quarterback the proper depth to drop to throw the football. Your players need to practice running a pattern many times before they'll feel confident that it will work.

Develop a game plan early in the week and then simplify it so that on game day you have only a handful of plays. By using a limited number of plays each week and giving the players enough repetitions to eliminate mistakes, you'll help your team execute consistently.

Move the Football

The object on offense is to move down the field and score by using a good mix of passing and running plays. Running basic plays against the defense you anticipate seeing is the best way to prepare your team to move the football in a game.

The offense must believe they can march the football down the field regardless of the team they're playing or the defense they're facing. Select plays that expose the defense's weakness and use the strengths of your offense.

Maintain Possession

Obviously, when the offense controls the football, the opponent cannot score. To keep control, the offense must consistently produce first downs. An offensive game of short, quick passes combined with effective running plays is hard to stop. Using a good mix of plays keeps the chains moving steadily toward the opponent's goal line.

Maintaining possession is especially important when your team has a narrow lead at the end of a game. The other team can't score if it doesn't get the ball.

Passing Game

The forward pass is a potent way to gain yardage and score points. Throwing the football helps develop individual players, forces the defense to defend the whole field, gains yardage on offense, and appeals to the crowd.

You must do a good job of drilling the quarterbacks and receivers in the basic skills covered later in this chapter. Keep the passing attack simple so that the quarterbacks and receivers know what to do. Timing is important to the success of a passing attack, so you must allow time in practice for players to perform many repetitions of the basic patterns.

The passing game starts with a pass tree (see figure 8.1). These are patterns that the receivers run to get open to catch the football. The quarterback drops straight back (or rolls out) and throws the football to the open receiver.

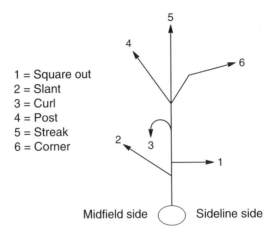

1 = Square out
2 = Slant
3 = Curl
4 = Post
5 = Streak
6 = Corner

Midfield side   Sideline side

Figure 8.1   Pass tree.

Here are the pass patterns we recommend you teach your players.

⊙ **Curl**—When the defensive player retreats too fast or is playing off the receiver, use the curl pattern. The receiver drives deep and then curls back to the football (see figure 8.2a).

⊙ **Square-out**—The square-out pattern is very successful when the defensive player is playing off the receiver (see figure 8.2b). The receiver runs downfield 5 to 10 yards and then cuts sharply to the sideline, catching the ball just before stepping out of bounds.

⊙ **Slant**—The slant is similar to a square-out, but the cut is not as sharp (see figure 8.2c). With this pattern you can often gain more yardage than with a square-out, though it can be a more difficult (longer) pass for a quarterback to throw.

⊙ **Streak**—Use the streak if the defensive back is playing tight on a receiver with speed. The receiver shows a curl move, then breaks to the outside and sprints downfield (see figure 8.2d).

⊙ **Post**—The post is similar to the streak, but the receiver breaks to the inside at an angle toward the center of the field (see figure 8.2e).

⊙ **Corner**—The corner (see figure 8.2f) is similar to a post, except the receiver breaks to the outside at an angle, toward a corner of the field.

The passing game takes time to develop, and you must be patient to bring the separate parts of this offense together.

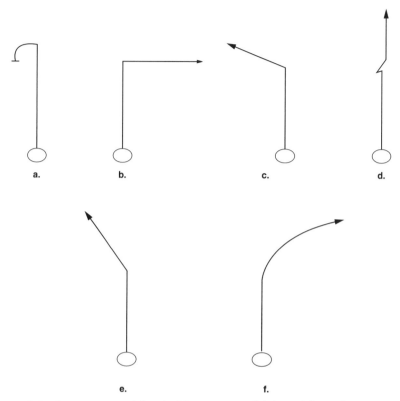

Figure 8.2   Pass patterns: *(a)* curl; *(b)* square-out; *(c)* slant; *(d)* streak; *(e)* post; *(f)* corner.

Passing Game

AIR BALL

Goal

To pass the ball down the field and score.

Description

Play 2 v 1 or 3 v 2 in a 20-yard-by-20-yard area (see figure 8.3). The quarterback tells the receiver(s) which routes to run. The offense begins on its goal line and gets three plays to advance the ball 20 yards. Give the offense one point for passing the 10-yard line and an additional point for passing the 20-yard line. The defense gets one point if the

(continued)

Air Ball *(continued)*

offense doesn't get past the 20-yard line and two points if it doesn't get past the 10-yard line. After a team advances past the 20-yard line, or after three plays, switch offense and defense, rotating players to maintain the offensive advantage.

To make the game easier:

- ⊙ Widen the area to 30 yards.
- ⊙ Play 4 v 2 or 5 v 3.

To make the game harder:

- ⊙ Play 2 v 2 or 3 v 3.
- ⊙ Make the field 15 yards wide and/or 30 yards deep.

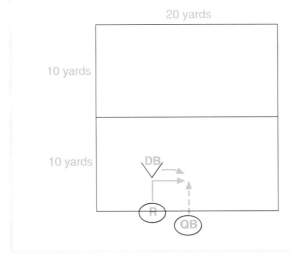

Figure 8.3 Air Ball.

Running Game

In flag and touch football, the running game is secondary because blocking is restricted and the number of line players is limited. Figure 8.4 shows a few plays that will help you open up a defense and make the players respect the run instead of just sitting back waiting for you to pass. The rules of flag and touch football do not permit double teams or two-on-one blocking.

In tackle football, you must develop an effective running game. The most important step is to design plays in which the blocking and

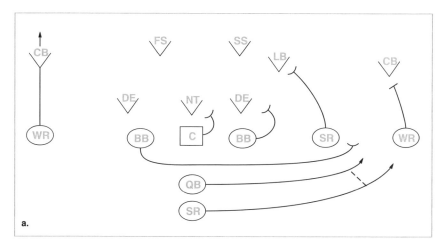

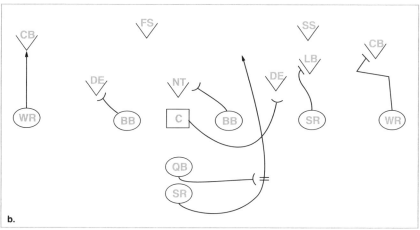

Figure 8.4 Two schemes for running plays in flag and touch football: (a) end sweep and (b) up the middle.

backfield action work together. The backfield action on any play must be designed to put the running back at the point of attack just as the hole is opening. Three types of blocks can help accomplish this: fast or quick blocking on straight-ahead plays, fold blocking on slower-hitting plays, and power blocking on sweeps. Figure 8.5 shows examples of the three types of blocking.

You should also set up the running game so that it is effective and easy to communicate. The simplest way to communicate running plays is to number each hole and back. Figure 8.6 shows how to do this in tackle football. The running back runs the ball into the hole that is called.

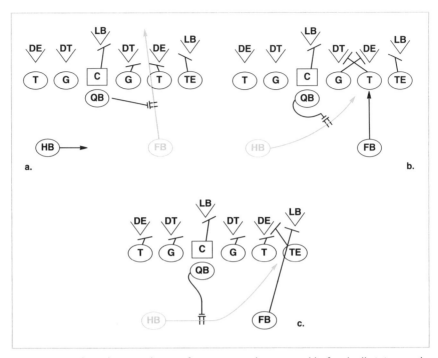

Figure 8.5 Three basic schemes for running plays in tackle football: (a) straight player-for-player block, (b) cross blocking, and (c) power blocking (double team).

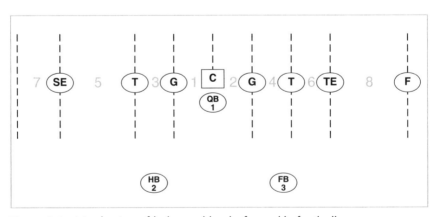

Figure 8.6 Numbering of holes and backs for tackle football.

For example, play 32 means that the number 3 back runs the ball through the number 2 hole. Figure 8.7 shows a similar numbering system for flag and touch football.

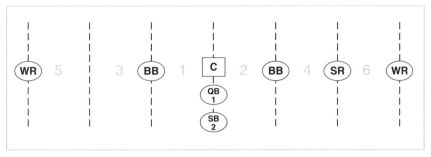

Figure 8.7   Numbering of holes and backs for flag and touch football.

In developing a running game, you should consider different series of plays that can all be successful. All series should include built-in dimension—that part of a given series that provides for variation of backfield movement. Dimension makes it difficult for the defense to determine the point of attack when the ball is snapped. This forces the defense to respect your entire attack. An example of a series is a dive 30 and a trap 30. These both involve the number 3 back running through the hole right in the center of the line, but the back gets there by different actions and the blocking is different.

The running game should give you the opportunity to run the football in every offensive hole. By incorporating series of plays, you'll be able to run the various holes in more than one way. The game plan, however, should include only four or five running plays chosen from the total series of plays. These are the plays you will perfect for a given opponent.

Successful football teams use runs that are effective against the opponent they are playing. For example, if the defense is coming across the line of scrimmage very hard, you would use the trap series. Against a hard-charging defense, it is easier for an offensive line player to get an angle if a trap is called. Sometimes the defender will take himself out of (overrun) the play; other times he or she can be blocked from the side. Against a reading defense, the dive and sweep would be effective. If the defense stacks the line of scrimmage, you may be better off throwing the ball.

The running backs are an integral part of a good running offense. Coach them to gain yardage on every play. They should be competitive and have the desire to be successful. Running backs who are hard to tackle and who keep their feet driving will make you and your team winners.

Running Game

HIT THE HOLE

Goal

To move the ball down the field by running the ball.

Description

Play 4 v 3 in a 10-yard-by-10-yard playing area. Stand behind the defensive players to point where the ball is to be run; don't allow the defense to see where you are pointing. The play begins on one "goal line," 10 yards from the other "goal line."

A running back, with a ball, is lined up behind three line players. On the running back's signal, the play begins. The running back runs through the area where you have pointed and attempts to gain as many yards as possible (see figure 8.8). The offense has three chances to score. The next play begins where the ball carrier was tackled. If

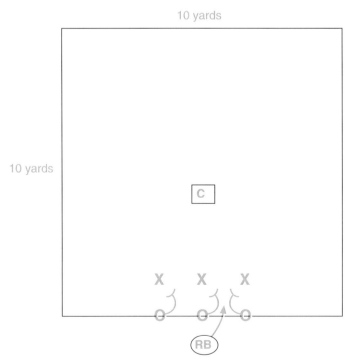

Figure 8.8   Hit the Hole.

the offense can "score" within the three plays, it gets a point. If it can't score, the defense gets a point. Switch offense and defense after the offense scores (or after it runs three plays), rotating players to maintain the 4 v 3 game. Let each offense have three different drives in which they try to score.

To make the game easier:
⊙ Widen the field to 15 or 20 yards wide.
⊙ Play 4 v 2.

To make the game harder:
⊙ Play 4 v 4.
⊙ Make the area 15 or 20 yards long.

Hurry-Up Offense

The hurry-up offense is designed to move the ball quickly down the field with no huddles. This means focusing on a mixture of your best passing plays, some short and some long.

Run-and-Shoot Offense

In this offense, the receivers respond to the defensive coverage and "shoot" to the open area. It's an exciting offense that calls for a quarterback with a strong arm and with an ability to find the open receiver, and for receivers who can read the defense and find the open seams on the field.

Defensive Tactics

Every defense has a purpose. You can design your defense to blitz, penetrate, pursue, contain, or perform any number of tactics to disrupt or stop the offense. Your defensive approach should reflect the talents of your players. Your basic defensive alignment must capitalize on their strengths and compensate for their weaknesses. For example, if you have a somewhat big, slow team, use more players on the line of scrimmage and try to control and contain the offense. If you have a small, quick team, use more linebackers and do more blitzing to take advantage of their quickness. Once you have determined your style of defense, stay with it.

The three most important goals a defense can strive to accomplish are

- ⊙ to prevent the easy touchdown,
- ⊙ to get possession of the ball, and
- ⊙ to score.

In addition, you'll want to teach your defense the basic concepts of playing an attacking defense, a pressure defense, and a contain defense. You'll also want to teach how to play player-to-player and zone defense. We'll look at the three goals first and then explore the different types of defenses.

Prevent the Easy Touchdown

Although the obvious objective on defense is to keep the opposition from scoring, a more functional objective of defensive play is to prevent the opposition from scoring the easy touchdown with a long pass or a long run. Make your opponent earn every point it scores by having a defense that challenges every yard. Praise players for preventing first downs and stopping the opponent's drives downfield.

Get Possession of the Ball

The defensive team may gain possession of the ball by preventing the opponent from gaining the next first down on four downs, forcing a punt, recovering a fumble, or intercepting a pass.

Score

The defense can score by returning a punt, a fumble, or an intercepted pass. (In flag football, all fumbles are dead at the spot to avoid pileups and subsequent injuries.) The defense also can score by downing the ball carrier in the offense's own end zone for a safety.

Attacking Defense

Use the following information to coach your defensive team to attack any running or passing game.

Alignments

If the offense is moving the ball, the defense must adjust alignment during the game to slow down the offense. For example, if the opponent is running the ball up the middle at your linebackers, switch to a defense that puts a defensive line player in the middle.

Proper Keys

A defensive skill that is more important at advanced levels is the ability to "read" what the offense is going to do before the ball is snapped. The obvious advantage in doing this is that your defenders will be able to anticipate the play and stop it. If you try to teach your players how to read the offense, keep the reads few and simple.

The most basic read is made by "keying" on an opponent's formation, tendencies in play selection, or individual player cues. For example, a defensive back may key on the offensive tackle or blocking back (flag and touch football) on his or her side of the field. If he or she sees the line player or blocking back set up to pass protect, the defensive back can assume it's a pass play and focus on covering his or her receiver. If the defensive back sees the line player or blocking back drive block, he or she can anticipate a running play and move into position to stop the ball carrier.

Flexibility

By having a knowledge of football and learning as much as you can about your defense's strengths and weaknesses, you will be able to make the proper adjustments during the game. The coach must prepare the defense to cover various formations and series of plays. For example, if you are running a three-deep secondary and the offense is passing the ball, you may want to go to the four-deep secondary.

If the offense gives you an unusual formation, your defensive players must know how to adjust. The offense's position on the field, the score, the time left in the game, and the type of offense your team is facing are all factors that influence the defense that you should run.

As the coach, you might consider limiting the defense according to the skill level of your team. It is more effective to run a few defenses well than to run many defenses poorly.

The individual skills that we talk about later in this chapter are good guidelines to incorporate into the total picture of a team defense. Team defense involves a group of players performing their individual techniques for the good of the team. Get the right players at the point of attack at the right time, and your team will be successful.

Defense Must Be Fun

Defensive football players are the aggressive kids who love to run and make contact. If you encourage emotion in defensive players, they will become excited when they make a tackle, touch, or flag pull; recover a fumble; or intercept a pass. This excitement adds to team unity, and the players will perform at a higher level.

In tackle football, encourage team tackling (where more than one person tackles the ball carrier). This motivates defensive players to swarm to the ball carrier and adds to team spirit. Stress hard work in an attempt to gain success, but make sure you add fun to the game.

Pressure Defense

The pressure defense is designed to force the offensive team into making mistakes. An example of this is when the defense forces the quarterback to throw the football before he or she is ready. Teach your defensive players the following points:

- A pressure defense uses a player-to-player pass coverage and tries to bump receivers as they start to run their patterns.
- The linebackers attack the line of scrimmage on the snap, trying to disrupt the offensive players' blocking schemes.
- In tackle football, the defensive alignment employs eight players within 5 yards of the line of scrimmage who can rush.
- In flag and touch football, the defensive alignment employs four players within 5 yards of the line of scrimmage who can rush.
- Defensive players can jump up into the line of scrimmage and then retreat. They can loop on their pass rush. They can rush two players through the same defensive hole to confuse the offense.

The pressure defense is a good strategy to use if you have confidence in your players' abilities and techniques. This is important because in this defense your defensive backs are isolated one on one with their receivers with no help from the safety.

The pressure defense changes the tempo of the game, preventing the opponent from retaining possession of the football and driving down the field. The pressure defense is a good change-up; use it when the offense is not expecting it. If you find a blitz that gives the offense trouble or that they cannot pick up, keep using it until they make the proper adjustment. Figure 8.9 shows a sample alignment for a pressure defense in tackle football. Figure 8.10 shows a sample alignment for flag and touch football.

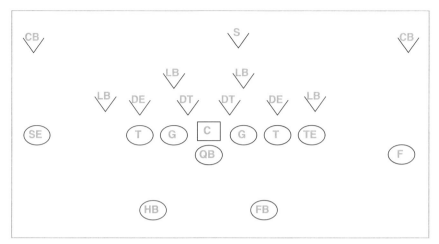

Figure 8.9 Alignment for a pressure defense in tackle football.

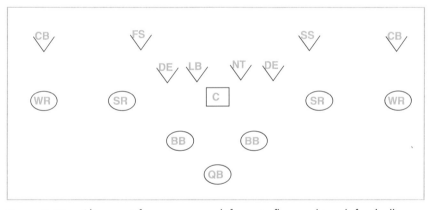

Figure 8.10 Alignment for a pressure defense in flag and touch football.

Pressure Defense Game

AIRTIGHT D

Goal

To stop the play at or behind the line of scrimmage.

Description

Play 2 v 2 or 3 v 3 in a 5-yard-wide by 10-yard-long playing area (see figure 8.11). The offense starts on its goal line and has three plays to make 10 yards. The defense gets one point for each time it prevents the offense from gaining any yardage. The offense has three downs to gain 10 yards and gets three points each time it does so. Rotate defense and offense when the offense gains 10 yards or when it has gone through its three plays.

To make the game easier:

- Play 2 v 3 or 3 v 4.
- Make the playing area 20 yards long.

To make the game harder:

- Play 3 v 2 or 4 v 3.
- Widen the field to 10 yards.

Figure 8.11   Airtight D.

Contain Defense

The contain defense plays a little softer than the pressure defense and tries to keep the offense from getting outside or deep. The defensive ends play for position to prevent ball carriers from getting outside them. After defensive players read their keys, they first control the gaps or areas of the field that they are responsible for and then react to the football. The defensive backs employ a zone coverage on passes to ensure that the receivers do not get behind them.

This type of defense requires disciplined players who carry out their assignments. It is effective in long-yardage situations just before the half and at the end of the game to ensure a victory.

Coaching is important to the success of a contain defense. The defensive players must recognize formations, types of running plays, and types of passes and must adjust to stop the play.

Contain Defense Game

LARGE AND IN CHARGE

Goal

To keep the offense from gaining 3 or more yards per play.

Description

Play 2 v 2 or 3 v 3 in a 5-yard-wide by 10-yard-long playing area (see figure 8.12). The offense starts on its goal line and has three plays to make 10 yards. The defense gets one point for each time it prevents the offense from gaining any yardage. The offense has three downs to gain 10 yards, and gets three points each time it does so. Rotate defense and offense when the offense gains 10 yards or when it has gone through its three plays.

The defense gets one point for each time it prevents the offense from gaining 3 or more yards. The offense has three downs to gain 10 yards. The offense gets three points each time it gains the 10 yards. After three plays (or after the offense scores), switch offense and defense.

To make the game easier:

- Play 2 v 3 or 3 v 4.
- Make the playing area 20 yards long.

(continued)

Large and in Charge *(continued)*

To make the game harder:

⊙ Play 3 v 2 or 4 v 3.

⊙ Widen the field to 10 yards.

5 yards

10 yards

Figure 8.12   Large and in Charge.

Player-to-Player Defense

In a player-to-player defense, each player on the defense is assigned a specific offensive player to cover. This defense works best when you have athletic players with speed and the ability to not get beat. In-experienced or slower players tend to get beat more often in one-on-one situations, leading to big gains or scores for the other team.

Think in terms of the team you are playing, too: If they have fast, athletic receivers, you may want to play a zone defense to lessen the risk of getting beat for a big play.

Zone Defense

In a zone defense, each defensive player is assigned to cover a certain area of the field. A zone can help guard against big plays; defensive help is never too far away. Mistakes made in zone defenses often are not as costly as those made in player-to-player defenses. A disadvantage of using a zone is that the opponent can overload a zone; in this case the defender in that zone should cover the deepest offensive player in the zone until the ball is thrown to a different player.

Special Teams

The special teams play an integral part in football. Sometimes players focus more on their duties on offense and defense and forget or downplay their roles as special teams players. Remind them that their contribution to special teams is important. You can help your special teams be successful by setting goals for them and by developing a successful strategy.

Goals for Special Teams

The main goal of the special teams is to perform their duties in such a way that they help the team win. You may want to consider some specific goals with your team:

- Know and adhere to the six don'ts:
  - ✔ Don't be offside.
  - ✔ Don't rough the kicker.
  - ✔ Don't clip.
  - ✔ Don't block below the waist.
  - ✔ Don't make mistakes.
  - ✔ Don't commit penalties that give the ball back to the offense or give them good field position.
- Win the battle of field position (on a kickoff, keep the opponents inside their 30-yard line). Good kicking and good coverage will accomplish this.
- Eliminate bad snaps.
- Make the big play (e.g., turnovers and blocked kicks).

Strategies for Special Teams

The kicking unit's primary objective is to execute the basic elements of the kicking game without making any big mistakes. Its second objective is to attack an opponent's weakness or exploit a situation when it arises.

The goal of special teams is to execute the basics. The punt coverage team must make sure the ball is kicked before they cover. Also, any time there is a return, the return team must avoid being the victim of a fake play by making sure that the other team has actually put the ball in the air.

By setting goals and developing a sound strategy, you can help make the kicking game a positive part of your flag football team.

Kicking Game Rules

- A player signals a fair catch by extending an arm above his or her head and waving it from side to side. The receiving player cannot hit or be hit after a fair catch.
- The kicking team may down the football after the ball has hit the ground.
- No one on either team may block below the waist.
- No player on the receiving team may touch the kicker unless the receiving team has blocked it and the kicker runs with the ball.
- A field goal is a scrimmage kick and uses the same rules as the punt.
- On a kickoff, after the ball has traveled 10 yards it is a free ball and either team can recover it (only in tackle football).

Offensive Skills

The offensive skills you will want to teach your players are stance, blocking, running the ball, playing quarterback, receiving, centering the ball, and kicking.

Stance

The stance is the proper alignment of a player's body to start each play. Following is a description of the stances you should teach players at each position.

Offensive Line Players

Before the snap, offensive line players should take a three-point stance. Figure 8.13 illustrates how this stance should look. Use these points to teach the correct stance to tackles, guards, and centers:

- Place the feet shoulder-width apart, in a heel-instep relationship, with the dominant foot back.
- Put very little weight on the down hand to allow for quick forward, backward, and lateral movement.

Figure 8.13   Proper three-point stance for an offensive line player.

- Place your left arm loosely across your left thigh.
- Keep your back straight, with your head up to see defenders across the line of scrimmage. This position is the strongest and safest for the back and neck.

Receivers

Receivers use two basic types of stances. The first is a three-point stance (tackle football), in which receivers distribute their weight evenly, with their heads up and eyes focused either directly downfield or on the football (see figure 8.14). The feet are staggered, which allows for good explosion from the line of scrimmage. The second stance used by wide receivers is a two-point or upright stance (see figure 8.15). This is used in tackle and flag and touch football. Its advantages are that receivers can get off the line of scrimmage without being held up and that they are in immediate position to receive quick passes.

Three-Point Stance.

- Place the feet shoulder-width apart, in a heel-toe relationship, with the foot closest to the football staggered in a comfortable sprinter's position.
- Point knees and toes straight ahead.
- Keep your back straight, parallel to the ground, and your head up.

Figure 8.14   Three-point stance for receivers.

Figure 8.15   Two-point stance for receivers.

Two-Point Stance.

- ⊚ Place the feet shoulder-width apart, in a heel-toe relationship, with the foot closest to the football back slightly more than the other.
- ⊚ Bend knees in a comfortable position.
- ⊚ Keep weight on the balls of your feet.
- ⊚ Keep your back straight, leaning forward slightly.
- ⊚ Square your shoulders to the line of scrimmage.
- ⊚ Hold your arms in a comfortable position.

Center

In flag and touch football, the center is an eligible pass receiver. He or she must be able to snap the ball back to the quarterback in a quick and accurate motion that will give the quarterback an extra second or two to read the defense and make a pass attempt or run with the ball. Centers must also be excellent receivers because they are in the center of the field and are involved in many pass plays. Centers are considered the tailback or workhorse of the offense in flag and touch football. They must also be able to pass protect on some occasions. Centers should use a three-point stance with their heads looking under their spread legs at the quarterback (see figure 8.16).

Figure 8.16   Three-point stance for centers.

- Place your feet shoulder-width apart in a heel-toe relationship, with the foot closest to the football staggered in a comfortable sprinter's position.
- Point knees and toes straight ahead.
- Keep your back straight, parallel to the ground, with your head looking back under your spread legs at the quarterback.

Quarterback

A quarterback's stance must be poised and relaxed, reflecting confidence. The quarterback's feet should be comfortably spread, approximately shoulder-width apart, and, in tackle football, as close to the center's feet as possible. Quarterbacks should bend their knees slightly and drop their hips while remaining as tall over the center as possible. Quarterbacks' shoulders should be parallel to the line of scrimmage, their heads up to check the positioning of the defense (see figure 8.17).

In flag and touch football, which are primarily passing games, quarterbacks usually stand in a shotgun formation to receive the snap. This gives them the advantage of being able to see the entire field and helps them separate from the line of scrimmage, giving them more time to throw.

Running Backs

The most common stance for halfbacks and fullbacks is a two-point stance (see figure 8.18). Players at these positions need to accelerate quickly from their backfield spot. Teach them to use the following stance before the ball is snapped:

- Place your feet about shoulder-width apart with your weight on the balls of your feet.
- Keep your feet nearly parallel for a quick burst in any direction.
- Bend your knees slightly and place your hands on your knees.
- Keep your head up and your eyes looking ahead.

If your running backs will be using the three-point stance, teach them the same stance technique you taught the offensive line players.

Blocking Backs

In flag and touch football, blocking backs have two roles—protecting the quarterback and receiving passes. They must be able to do both well. Blocking backs should start out in a two-point stance so that they

Figure 8.17 Quarter-back's stance.

Figure 8.18 Two-point stance for running backs.

can see oncoming defensive players. A two-point stance also enables a blocking back to release quickly into a pass pattern. Blocking backs need to accelerate quickly from their backfield spots. Teach them to use the stance you taught the running backs.

- ⊙ Place your feet about shoulder-width apart with your weight on the balls of your feet.
- ⊙ Keep your feet nearly parallel for a quick burst in any direction.
- ⊙ Bend your knees slightly and place your hands on your knees.
- ⊙ Keep your head up and your eyes looking ahead.

Blocking

Blocking is the cornerstone of all successful offensive teams. Teams use blocking to move a defensive player out of the area where they want to run the football and to keep defensive line players from tackling, touching, or pulling the flag of the quarterback.

In tackle football, offensive line players block in some manner on every play. Running backs block when they are not carrying the football, and wide receivers block when they are not catching the football. In flag and touch football, blocking backs block on every play. Wide receivers block when they are not catching the ball.

Teach your players these blocks: the drive block, the downfield block, and the pass protection block. In flag and touch football, also instruct your players in contact and screen blocking. All blocking in flag and touch football is done from a two-point stance with an open-hand, straight-arm approach.

Drive Block

The drive block is a one-on-one block used most often when a defensive line player lined up directly over an offensive player must be moved for the play to succeed. When teaching your tackle football players the drive block, emphasize these points (see figure 8.19):

- ⊙ Explode from your stance with the foot closest to the opponent and drive your hips forward on the third and fourth steps through the block.
- ⊙ Start with short, choppy steps and keep your feet moving.
- ⊙ Deliver the block from a wide base; and keep your head up and shoulders square.

Figure 8.19   Proper drive blocking position for tackle football.

⊚ Punch hands into the opponent to establish momentum; and deliver the blow on impact with the hands on forearms, not the head.

⊚ Keep your head on the side of the opponent toward the hole; and follow through with short, choppy steps, turning the opponent away from the hole.

In teaching your flag and touch football players the drive block, emphasize these points (see figure 8.20):

⊚ Start with short, choppy steps and keep your feet moving, your head up, and your hands and arms out in front of your body to keep the defensive player away from you.

⊚ Deliver the block from a wide base and keep your head up and shoulders square.

⊚ Keep your head on the side of the opponent toward the hole; and follow through with short, choppy steps, turning the opponent away from the hole.

Figure 8.20   Proper drive blocking position for flag and touch football.

Drive Blocking Game

DRIVE-THROUGH

Goal

To use drive blocking to open holes for the ball carrier.

Description

Play 3 v 2 or 4 v 3 in a 5-square-yard area (see figure 8.21). The game begins with the offensive line's first move. The offense gets one point every time it keeps the defense from tackling the ball carrier. The defense gets one point each time it tackles the ball carrier. Each team gets three consecutive plays. Rotate players to keep the advantage with the same number of blockers and defenders.

To make the game easier:

⊙ Make the playing field wider.

⊙ Have the defense play at half or three-quarters speed.

To make the game harder:
  ⊙ Make the field narrower.
  ⊙ Have the defense play at full speed.

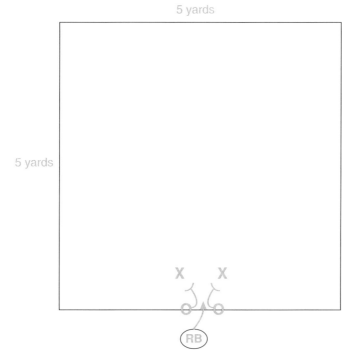

Figure 8.21   Drive-Through.

Downfield Block

Downfield blocks must be made above the defender's waist. Teach your players two kinds of downfield blocks. In tackle football, blockers should use the run-block technique when the ball carrier is directly behind them. In this situation, they block the defender at full or three-quarter speed by attacking aggressively with the forearms and shoulders. In touch and flag football, players block the defender at full or three-quarter speed with an arms-extended, open-palms approach to the upper body of the opponent.

Downfield Blocking Game

THE ESCORT

Goal

To gain yards by blocking downfield for the ball carrier.

Description

Play 2 v 1 or 3 v 2 in a 10-square-yard wide area (see figure 8.22). Have blockers and defenders start at least 5 yards apart. The game begins with the blocker's first move. The offense gets one point every time it keeps the defense from tackling the ball carrier. The defense gets one point each time it tackles the ball carrier. Switch offense and defense after three plays, rotating players to keep the same numbers on offense and defense.

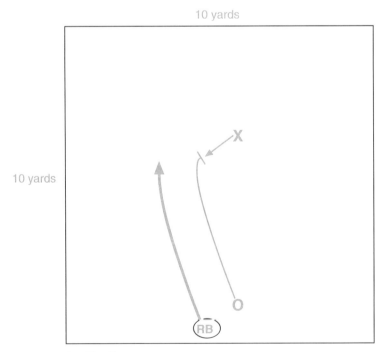

Figure 8.22   The Escort.

To make the game easier:
- Make the playing field wider.
- Play 3 v 1 or 4 v 2.

To make the game harder:
- Make the field narrower.
- Play 2 v 2 or 3 v 3.

Pass Protection Block

The pass protection block keeps the defender from getting to the quarterback before the quarterback can throw the football. Teach your running backs and your offensive line players (in tackle football) and your blocking backs (in flag and touch football) the same technique for protecting the quarterback. Use the following sequential method to teach the pass protection block.

Initial Move and Setup. The initial move and setup technique is extremely important in pass blocking. In tackle football, the line player must set up quickly, stepping with his or her inside foot first. The offensive line player pushes up into a two-point stance with the down hand. The movement projects the offensive line player into a position with the head up, eyes open wide, back straight, rear end down, hand and arms up, and feet positioned to move back or laterally in a split second. The depth behind the line of scrimmage should vary with the pass action called and the opponent's defensive front alignment.

Blocking backs in flag and touch football use the same technique except that they start in a two-point stance with both hands on their knees.

Body Position.

- Keep your head up and your rear end down.
- Keep your back straight.
- Place your feet shoulder-width apart, keep them moving, and flex your knees.
- Keep the weight of your body and head over your feet, never in front of them.
- Hold your elbows in with the hands inside your shoulders, ready to ward off the challenge of the defensive line player.

Line players must position themselves between the quarterback and the defensive pass rusher. They can do this by backing off the line of scrimmage quickly after the snap. Tell your offensive line players that they should never get beat to their inside.

Blocking backs must also position themselves between the quarterback and the defensive rusher. They can do this by backing off the line of scrimmage quickly after the snap or by setting up a few yards deep in the backfield before the snap.

Punch. It takes good timing to deliver a blow to stop the charge of the defensive line player. The player must let the defensive line player get as close as six inches and then deliver the blow to stop the charge. The line player or blocking back must strive to deliver a blow, step back from the defensive line player, and recoil. The player must deliver the punch with the elbows locked and close to the rib cage and rolling the wrists to get power. No, we aren't recommending that you teach your line players or blocking backs to throw left hooks at charging defenders. The line players' or blocking backs' hands and arms must stay within the planes of the shoulders.

Patience. Patience may be the hardest thing to teach offensive line players or blocking backs. They must be the protector, not the aggressor. They must keep their legs under them and always remain in a good blocking position even after delivering the punch. An effective coaching point is to instruct line players or blocking backs to keep their rear ends down and their knees bent at all times.

Footwork. The most important skill for offensive line players or blocking backs is the ability to move their feet. The correct foot movement is a shuffle, with the player keeping one foot always in contact with the ground. The line players or blocking backs should never cross their feet and should keep their bodies parallel to the line of scrimmage with their backs always to the quarterback. Blockers should keep their feet shoulder-width apart. Figure 8.23 shows the proper position for pass protection.

Figure 8.23   Proper position for pass protection.

Pass Blocking Game

PROTECTING THE QB

Goal

To keep defensive players from getting to the quarterback.

Description

Play 2 v 1 or 3 v 2 in a 5-square-yard area: a quarterback and one or two line players on offense and one or two defensive line players. The offense and defense start opposite each other at one of the 5-yard marks. You stand behind the defense and signal the start count to the offense. On the count the blocker(s) move into pass protection blocking as the quarterback drops back to pass (see figure 8.24). The blockers must keep the defensive players from getting to the quarterback for

(continued)

Protecting the QB *(continued)*

at least 5 seconds. The offense gets one point for keeping the defense away from the quarterback. The defense gets one point for touching the quarterback.

To make the game easier:

- Give the defense only 3 seconds to touch the quarterback.
- Play 3 v 1 or 4 v 2.

To make the game harder:

- Give the defense 7 seconds to touch the quarterback.
- Play 2 v 2 or 3 v 3.

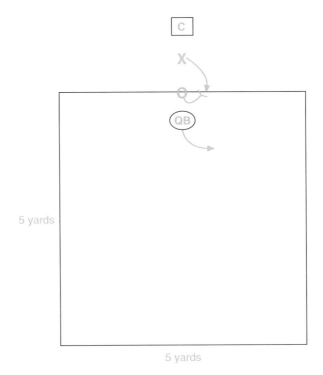

Figure 8.24 Protecting the QB.

Hook Block

The hook block is used when executing sweeps. The blocker (usually the end in this case) seals off the opposing end so the running back can run around the end to the outside. The blocker makes contact and then steps with the outside foot and swings around to contain the rusher (see figure 8.25).The blocker hits the defender at or slightly above waist level and keeps the point of contact to the side on which the sweep is being run.

Cross Block

The cross block can be used as an element of surprise, to adjust for a mismatch at the line of scrimmage, or to block against a defensive alignment that is difficult to block straight on. Blocking form and execution are the same as in the open-the-hole block, except for the timing between the blockers. Cross blocks can be performed by teammates who line up next to each other—a center and guard, a guard and tackle, a tackle and tight end (or, in flag football, a center and end) (see figure 8.26). This is a bang-bang play; timing and explosive power are the keys.

a

Figure 8.25   Hook block *(a-c)*.   *(continued)*

b

Figure 8.25   *(continued)*

c

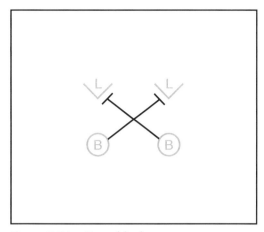

Figure 8.26   Cross block.

Contact Blocking

Contact blocking in flag and touch football is legally hindering the progress of an opponent in a fair and safe way. Blockers must be on their feet before, during, and after they make contact with their opponents. In flag and touch football, the following play is not allowed anywhere on the field by a blocker:

- Diving to block
- Two-on-one blocking
- High-low block, cross-body block, or rolling block
- Grabbing the jersey of an opponent while attempting to block
- Locking the hands together
- Swinging, throwing, or flipping the elbow or forearm
- Contact of any kind to the head or shoulders

The blocker is allowed to contact the opponent's body only between the waist and shoulders. An open-hand, straight-arm block within the framework of the blocker's body is the ideal block to use to avoid unnecessary rough play. To keep contact blocking under control, stress safe, clean, sportsmanlike contact between opponents.

Screen Blocking

In flag and touch football, screen blocking is legally obstructing an opponent without making contact with any part of the body. Screen blockers may have their hands and arms at the side or behind the back;

any use of the arms, elbows, or legs to initiate contact during a screen block is illegal. Blockers may use their hands or arms to break a fall or retain their balance. Players must be on their feet before, during, and after screen blocking. Several restrictions govern screen blocking:

1. When behind a stationary opponent, a screening player may not take a position closer than a normal step from the opponent.

2. When assuming a position at the side or in front of a stationary opponent, a screening player may not make contact with the opponent.

3. A screen blocker may not take a position so close to a moving opponent that the opponent cannot avoid contact by stopping or changing direction. The speed of the player to be screened will determine where the screener may take a stationary position. This position will vary and may be one or two normal steps or strides from the opponent.

4. After assuming a legal screening position, screen blockers may not move to maintain it unless they move in the same direction and path as the opponent. If screeners violate any of these provisions and contact results, they have committed a personal foul.

Blocking and Interlocked Interference. Teammates of a runner or passer may interfere for the player by screen blocking, but may not use interlocked interference by grasping or encircling one another in any manner.

Use of Hands or Arms by the Defense. Defensive players must go around the offensive player's screen block. They may not use the arms and hands as a wedge to contact the opponent. The application of this rule depends entirely on the judgment of the official. Blockers may use their arms or hands to break a fall or retain their balance.

Screen Blocking Game

SCREEN DOOR

Goal

To use screen blocking to keep defenders from the ball carrier.

Description

Play 4 v 2 in an area 10 yards wide. On offense have a quarterback, running back, and two blockers; on defense have defensive backs.

The quarterback begins with the ball; on the quarterback's signal the play begins and the running back receives a swing pass in the flat (see figure 8.27). The running back then follows his or her blockers and tries to elude the defenders. Give the offense one point each time the back is able to elude the defenders by using the blockers. Rotate players every three plays.

To make the game easier:

- Widen the field.
- Play 4 v 1 or 5 v 2.

To make the game harder:

- Narrow the field.
- Play 4 v 3.

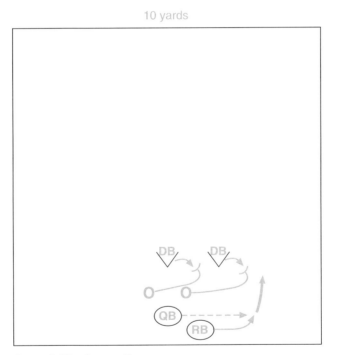

Figure 8.27   Screen Door.

Blocking Game

FOLLOW THE LEADER

Goal

For ball carriers to use blockers as a shield between themselves and defenders.

Description

Play 2 v 1 in a 10-yard-by-10-yard area. Blockers use a hand behind their back to signal which way the ball carrier should go and on what count. Ball carriers are behind the blockers with the ball in their hands. The blocker lines up on one of the 10-yard markers and the play begins on the blocker's first move (see figure 8.28). The offense gets one point each time it gains 10 or more yards in one play. The defense gets one point each time it stops the offense from gaining 10 or more

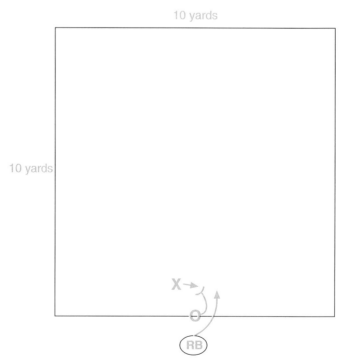

Figure 8.28 Follow the Leader.

yards. Rotate players after a running back has run three straight times with the ball.

To make the game easier:

- Make the area wider.

To make the game harder:

- Make the area narrower.
- Play 3 v 2 or 4 v 3.

Running the Ball

Running the ball involves many skills, including getting the handoff, carrying the ball, and using blockers.

Getting the Handoff

Instruct running backs that when they are getting the handoff from the quarterback, the elbow of the inside arm (the arm closest to the quarterback) should be up to receive the ball. They should bend the inside arm at the elbow (90-degree angle) and keep it parallel to the ground at about shoulder level. They should place the outside arm (the arm farthest from the quarterback) across the belt with the elbow close to the body, the palm of the hand turned up, and the fingers spread. Figure 8.29 shows a running back in proper handoff position. The quarterback places the football into the pocket formed by the running back.

Carrying the Football

After receiving the ball, backs must protect it at all cost. Teach ball carriers to immediately tuck the end of the ball under the arm and cover the front point of the ball with the hand. The players should carry the ball away from the pressure of the defense. When ball carriers are running to the right, the ball should be in the right arm, and when they're running to the left, the ball should be in the left arm. The hand the ball is in should always be over the point. Coach your players to carry the ball in the arm away from the defense.

Using Blockers

Coach your backs to run toward the hole that has been called unless they see that the hole is closed. They should then head upfield to gain what yardage they can. Teach them to run with a forward lean. This helps them to stay low and have a good forward drive.

Figure 8.29   Running back in proper handoff position.

Instruct the backs to make their cut at the last moment. They should approach the line of scrimmage with their shoulders square to the line. To prevent the defender from getting a solid bead, a good running back will fake the defender by taking a step away from him or her and then cutting back close to the defender as if the ball carrier were cutting right through the defender. Coach backs to set up their blockers by running on the blocker's outside hip, and then, at the last moment, cutting inside as the blocker blocks the defender.

Playing Quarterback

You'll need to teach your quarterbacks how to take snaps from center, play out of the shotgun formation, hand off, throw laterals, and throw passes.

Taking the Snap From Under the Center

Quarterbacks should place their throwing hand, or pressure hand, so that it pushes up on the center's rear end. This pressure tells the center where to snap the football. Quarterbacks should position the bottom hand, or catch hand, so that the thumbs are together and the fingers extended, giving the center a good target for the ball. Quarterbacks should bend their elbows slightly to allow for the center's firing out on the snap.

At first, centers should practice snapping the ball slowly to the quarterback, making sure they are getting it properly with the laces at or near the fingers of the throwing hand. The players should then practice at full speed. Spend five minutes each day on center-quarterback exchanges. Figure 8.30 illustrates a quarterback receiving the snap.

The quarterback looks downfield and, after receiving the snap, turns his or her head to see where to hand off the ball. When quarterbacks locate their target, they should keep their eyes on that player. On passing plays, they bring the football into their body at the chest and then raise it up to the ear in a ready-to-throw position. The quarterback should not swing the football.

Figure 8.30   Quarterback receiving a snap.

Shotgun Formation

Quarterbacks start in the shotgun formation—that is, about 5 to 7 yards behind the center, depending on the particular play or their arm strength. They should look at the defense and scan the field for particular defensive formations. That will enable them to see who might be open or alert them to call an audible if the defensive set indicates that a change of play is needed.

Handoff

Quarterbacks are completely responsible for the success or failure of the handoff. They must adjust to the backs' paths and speed and get them the football.

Instruct quarterbacks to keep both hands on the ball as long as possible and to place or press the ball firmly into the ball carrier's stomach, allowing the give hand to ride the ball into place until the running back takes it.

Laterals and Pitches

Instruct your players to use a two-hand push pass on all pitch plays (see figure 8.31a). Remind running backs to look the ball into their hands and not try to run with the ball until they have caught it. The running back's hands should be wide open, with the thumbs together, in preparing to catch the ball (see figure 8.31b-c). Upon catching it, the back should secure it and head upfield.

A lateral is an overhand pass that is not a forward pass: It is thrown either to the side (thus the name lateral) or back (in relation to the line of scrimmage), rather than forward. A dropped lateral is not an incomplete pass; it is a dead ball in flag and touch football, and a fumble in tackle football.

Throwing the Football

Throwing for quarterbacks really entails four aspects: the grip, the throwing position, the release, and the follow-through.

The Grip. Spread the fingers over the laces of the ball by contacting the laces with the fingers. Hold the ball slightly back of center. Make sure the grip is secure. Keep the ball in the ready position, close to your armpit, before raising it straight up to throw. Figure 8.32 shows the proper grip with the ball in the ready position.

The Throwing Position. Bring the ball with both hands to the throwing position just behind the ear. Move the nonpassing hand away and in front of the ball. The upper arm of the passing arm is about parallel to the ground. The nonpassing shoulder (left shoulder for a right-handed passer) is pointing to the intended receiver. Legs are about shoulder-width apart with the weight partially on the back foot. Figure 8.33 shows a quarterback in proper throwing position.

The Release. Throw the ball from behind the ear, releasing it with a strong wrist snap, with the palm turned down toward the ground (see figure 8.34). As the ball is being released, drag the fingers across it to

a

b

c

Figure 8.31 Proper hand placement on the pitch.

Figure 8.32 Proper grip—ball in ready position.

Figure 8.33 Proper throwing position for a quarterback.

Figure 8.34   Proper release.

cause it to spiral. The index finger is the last to leave the ball and should be pointed directly toward the target.

The Follow-Through. Keep the passing arm from going down across the body too quickly. Try to make the hand "follow the ball" to the target (see figure 8.35).

Passing Games

Try the game "Screen Door" on page 128 and the game "Air Ball" on page 95.

Figure 8.35   Following through.

Receiving

Receiving involves running patterns and catching the football.

Running Routes

When the quarterback calls a play in the huddle, the receiver knows what route to run. The quarterback selects a play that uses routes from many options on a pass tree (see figure 8.1 on page 94).

The most important thing you should teach receivers is to explode off the line of scrimmage. They should run to the outside shoulder of the defensive back, forcing defenders to turn their shoulders parallel to the line of scrimmage to cover them. Next, receivers must come under control at the breaking point of the route. They then plant a foot, turn the head and shoulders, and react to the football.

Catching the Football

The next step in coaching receivers is to teach them how to catch the football. This is a matter of concentration and dedication. Receivers should watch the football into their hands. If the football is thrown high, receivers should catch it with thumbs together (see figure 8.36a); if it is

Figure 8.36 *(a)* Catching a high ball; *(b)* catching a low ball; *(c)* catching with the hands, away from the body.

thrown low, receivers should catch it with little fingers together (see figure 8.36b). Also, you must teach receivers to catch the football in their hands and not trap it against their bodies (see figure 8.36c).

Give receivers ample opportunities to catch every type of pass that they will see in games. As a coach, you cannot expect athletes to perform skills in a game that you have not worked on in practice. Instruct receivers to tuck the ball under the arm and protect it after making the catch. Success will help the receivers gain confidence, and first downs and touchdowns reinforce that catching the ball is fun.

Catching Game

CATCHING ON

Goal

To catch the ball.

Description

Play 2 v 1 or 3 v 2 in an area 10 yards wide (see figure 8.37). The quarterback tells the receiver(s) what route to run and the count to start on. The play begins on the quarterback's count and each offense gets three consecutive plays. The offense gets one point each time it completes a pass and the defense gets one point each time it prevents a receiver from catching the ball. Rotate players after every three consecutive plays.

To make the game easier:
- Move receiver(s) closer to the quarterback.
- Play 3 v 1 or 4 v 2.
- Have the defense play at half speed.

To make the game harder:
- Move receiver(s) farther from the quarterback.
- Play 2 v 2 or 3 v 3.
- Have the defense play at full speed.

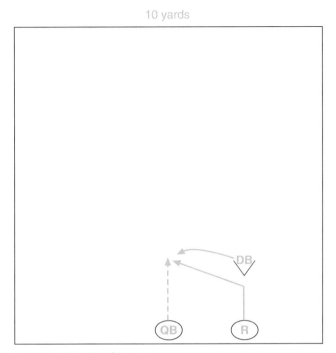

Figure 8.37 Catching On.

Centering the Ball

Players at the center position will need to learn how to center the ball in two formations: a tight formation and the shotgun formation.

In the tight formation, the quarterback is lined up directly behind the center, with his or her hands open and ready to receive the ball directly from the center. At one point in the ball exchange, both the center's hands and the quarterback's hands will be touching the ball (see figure 8.30 on page 133). The snap should be hard and direct, going through the center's legs and into the quarterback's waiting hands.

In the shotgun formation, the center snaps the ball through his or her legs to the quarterback, who is 5 to 7 yards behind the line of scrimmage. The snap should be crisp, but not so fast that it is hard to handle. The ball should come to the quarterback at about the middle of the chest, with a nice spiral so that it is easy to grab.

Kicking Game

The kicking game is an important part of football. About one-fourth of the game involves kicking, so you definitely need to spend time on it. Three phases of the kicking game that we address in this chapter are the punt, the placekick, and the kickoff.

The Punt

The punt is used on fourth down to turn the ball over to the opponent. The punting team's objective is to give the opponent a less-favorable field position. Coach your kickers to follow these guidelines to punt successfully.

- Line up 10 yards behind the center.
- Assume a comfortable stance with knees slightly bent and arms extended (see figure 8.38a).
- When you drop the ball, there should be no movement at the elbows, wrists, or shoulders.

a   b

Figure 8.38   Proper kicking technique for a punter *(a-d)*.

c   d

Figure 8.38   (continued)

○ Drop the ball parallel to the ground with the tip turned slightly in (see figure 8.38b).

○ Your foot speed is not as important as making proper contact on the center of the ball (see figure 8.38c).

○ The nonkicking leg should remain in contact with the ground.

○ Allow the kicking leg to extend and follow through after the kick (see figure 8.38d).

The key to coaching punters is to teach them correct technique and then allow them to practice and develop their rhythm. They should strive for consistency in height and distance.

Punting Game

FIELD POSITION

Goal

To gain better field position than the other team through returning punts and defending against returned punts.

Description

Play 3 v 3 in a 15-yard-wide-by-50-yard-deep area (see figure 8.39). Team A (who will punt first) lines up on the 10-yard line and punts to team B, who returns the punt as far as possible. Team B then lines up at the point they were tackled and punts the ball back to team A, who returns the ball as far as they can. Play continues in this fashion until each team has made three punts. The team with the best field position wins the game.

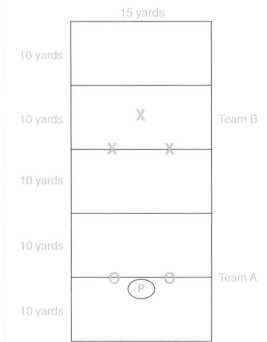

Figure 8.39 Field Position.

To make the game easier for offense (and harder for defense):
- ⊙ Widen the field.
- ⊙ Put an additional player on the receiving team.

To make the game harder for offense (and easier for defense):
- ⊙ Make the field narrower.
- ⊙ Put an additional player on the punting team.

Covering Punts.   Punt coverage involves organizing your punt team so that they can cover the punt and down the ball carrier before he or she can advance the ball upfield. The punter should kick the ball for distance and keep it in the air long enough to give the coverage team time to get downfield and make the play. Figure 8.40 shows a common punt coverage team alignment for tackle football; figure 8.41 shows a common alignment for flag and touch football. In both coverages, the two outside line players are contain players; they must not let anyone outside them. All other players should always stay in their lanes and let the ball come to them.

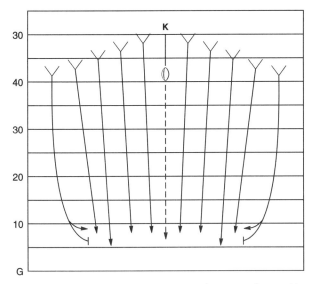

Figure 8.40   Punt coverage team alignment for tackle football.

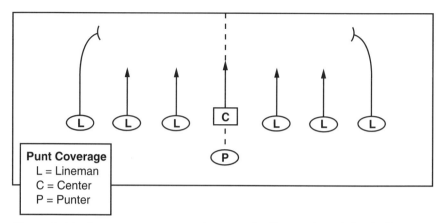

Figure 8.41 Punt coverage team alignment for flag and touch football.

Returning Punts. In receiving punts in tackle football, use either one or two players back to return the punt. In flag and touch football, it's best to use one player back to receive the punt (see figure 8.42). Then, if the opposition fakes the punt and runs a play, the defense will be ready to defend. Once a punt is made, the three defensive backs in the middle drop back to form a V. The safety, after catching the ball, should take it up the middle.

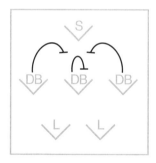

Figure 8.42   Formation for returning punts: flag and touch football.

The Placekick

The two basic types of placekicking are straight-ahead style and soccer style. Both are effective. Have your kickers follow these coaching points, regardless of the kicking style they use.

- Stand three steps behind where the ball will be placed (and one-and-a-half to two steps to the side for soccer style). Your kicking foot should be slightly behind your nonkicking foot and your eyes should be on the spot where the ball will be placed.
- Take a short step with the nonkicking leg and then a slightly longer than normal step with your kicking leg (see figures 8.43a-b).
- Plant your nonkicking foot about a shoe's length away from the ball, to the side of the ball (see figure 8.43c). This foot should be pointed at the middle of the goalposts.
- Bend your kicking leg behind your body and use a smooth swing.
- Point your toe for a smooth, hard surface. Contact the ball on the large bone on top of the foot. The point of contact should be about 4 inches above the lower end of the ball.
- Use a full follow-through. Finish with your leg in line with your opposite shoulder (see figure 8.43d).

Give kickers the opportunity to practice kicking in game-like situations.

a *b*

(continued)

Figure 8.43   *(a)* First step: short. *(b)* Second step: longer than normal. *(c)* The plant. *(d)* Finishing with the follow-through.

c   d

Figure 8.43   *(continued)*

Placekicking Game

TRIFECTA

Goal

To kick the ball from a placekicking tee through the goalpost uprights.

Description

Play 5 v 2 or 7 v 4 with the ball placed 13 yards from the goalposts (see figure 8.44). The play starts when the center hikes the ball to the placekick holder. The defensive players cannot hit the center, but they can attempt to block the kick. The kicking team gets three points for each successful kick. Each team gets three consecutive kicks.

To make the game easier:

- Make the kick shorter.
- Have the holder start with the ball in his or her hands; the play starts when he or she moves to place it on the tee.

To make the game harder:

- ⊙ Make the kick longer.
- ⊙ Add a defensive player.
- ⊙ Move the ball to the left or right hash marks.

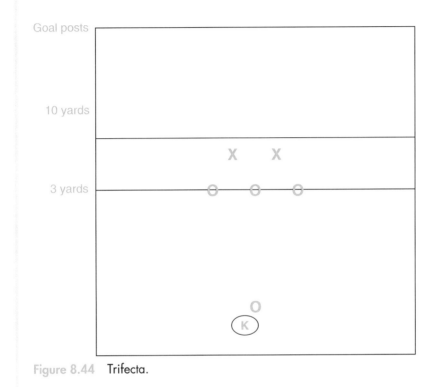

Figure 8.44 Trifecta.

The Kickoff

The main difference between the kickoff and the placekick is in the approach phase of the kick. A longer approach run is used on the kickoff, allowing the kicker to build up more speed and momentum before the kick.

Kickers line up 5 to 10 yards from the football. As they approach the ball, they must adjust their steps so that they run through the ball without slowing. The key coaching point on the kickoff is for kickers to make contact with the ball and work on being consistent. The two outside line players are contain players; they must not let anyone outside them. The kicker/safety back should hang back to prevent any long return from becoming a touchdown. All other players should stay in their lanes and let the ball come to them.

In returning kickoffs, you might consider employing various strategies. Here are diagrams showing three such strategies for flag and touch football: up the middle (see figure 8.45), down the sideline (see figure 8.46), and the reverse (see figure 8.47). You can adapt them for tackle football.

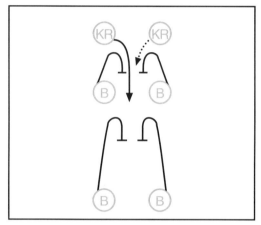

Figure 8.45   Up-the-middle strategy.

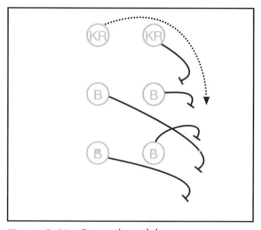

Figure 8.46   Down-the-sideline strategy.

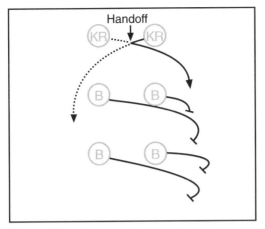

Figure 8.47   Reverse strategy.

Kickoff Game

KICKING INTO GEAR

Goal

To gain better field position than the other team through returning kickoffs and defending against kickoffs.

Description

Play 3 v 3 in a 15-yard-wide-by-50-yard-deep area (see figure 8.48). Team A (who will kick off first, using a tee) lines up on the 10-yard line and kicks off to team B, who returns the kickoff as far as possible. Team B then lines up at the point they were tackled and kicks off back to team A, who returns the ball as far as they can. Play continues in this fashion until each team has made three kickoffs. The team with the best field position wins the game.

To make the game easier for offense (and harder for defense):

- Widen the field.
- Put an additional player on the receiving team.

(continued)

Kicking into Gear *(continued)*

To make the game harder for offense (and easier for defense):
- ⊙ Make the field narrower.
- ⊙ Put an additional player on the kicking team.

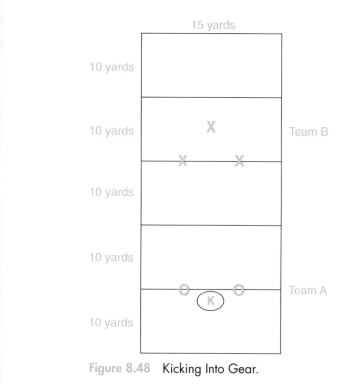

Figure 8.48   Kicking Into Gear.

Defensive Skills

Playing defense is part instinct, part effort, and part technique. You can't do much about your players' instincts, and most young players love the game, so effort isn't a problem. What you *can* do is teach and develop players' defensive skills. The rest of this chapter will focus on defensive stance, tackling (pulling the flag or touching), rushing the passer, and covering receivers.

Stance

The proper initial alignment of the body for the defensive player is very important. Teach the defensive line players, linebackers, and defensive backs the proper stances for their respective positions.

Defensive Line Players

The typical stance for defensive line players is similar to the offensive line player's three-point stance (see figure 8.13 on page 111). However, in tackle football some defensive line players are more comfortable with the outside hand on the ground, creating a four-point stance as shown in figure 8.49. Give your players the following pointers:

- Place more weight on your hands so that you can move forward.
- Use a stance that is a little wider so that you have better balance when you're being blocked.
- Keep your outside hand (the hand away from the blocker) free to try pass rush techniques and to keep from getting hooked.
- Keep your body low to the ground and control the line of scrimmage from underneath the opponent's shoulder pads (tackle football).
- Keep your body low to the ground and use your speed and quickness to get by the blocking backs (flag and touch football).
- Use a spin move or a stutter step to help you keep the blocker off balance.

Figure 8.49 Four-point stance for defensive line players.

Linebackers

Linebackers should have a good balanced stance, which means that their feet are shoulder-width apart and slightly staggered. Figure 8.50 shows the proper stance for a linebacker. Teach your linebackers the following points:

- ⊙ Bend your knees slightly to ensure low body position, with your hands on your upper thighs.
- ⊙ Focus your eyes on the player you are to get the key from.
- ⊙ Have one foot slightly forward; step with this foot first as you react to the key and find the football.

Figure 8.50 Proper stance for linebackers.

Defensive Backs

Coach the defensive backs to line up with a slightly staggered stance in a relaxed position. Figure 8.51 shows the proper stance for a defensive back. Instruct your players as follows:

- ⊙ Keep your feet slightly staggered, with the outside foot back.
- ⊙ Point the toes straight ahead.

Figure 8.51 Proper stance for defensive backs.

- Focus eyes on the player you are to key.
- Assume a slightly crouching position with your knees bent a little.
- Take a short read step on the snap, and then react to the play.

Tackling

If you want to have a good defensive team, you must teach your defensive players to tackle. Players who are just beginning to learn the game may only be able to get into a position to grab ball carriers and pull them down, but as the players grow and progress, it is important that you teach them the proper techniques of tackling.

Tacklers should always be in the proper hitting position and have a target to focus on in making the tackle (this is usually the area of the runner's belt buckle). If tacklers focus on this target, their opponent will not be able to fake them out with a fancy shoulder move. The three basic tackles that your players will be using are the head-on tackle, the angle tackle, and the open-field tackle. Here are some coaching points for each type.

Head-On Tackle

Defensive players use the head-on tackle when they line up straight across from the offensive runner coming toward them. Tacklers should first make sure they are in a good hitting position and are ready to make the tackle. Emphasize the following points to your tacklers:

- Make sure that you are under control so as not to overrun the ball carrier or dive and miss the tackle.
- Maintain a wide, balanced stance; keep the feet moving with choppy steps.
- Extend your arms and head in front of your body.
- Keep your head up, your back arched, and your knees slightly bent.
- A head-on tackle means the ball carrier is coming straight toward you. It does not mean you should lead with your head! Slide your head to the outside before making contact.
- Drive your shoulder into the runner's abdomen as you thrust your hips through.
- With your arms, grasp behind the legs of the ball carrier and pull him or her toward you.
- Lift and pull ball carriers toward you as you take them off their feet.

Figure 8.52 shows proper tackling technique. This is the tackle technique that you should teach your young athletes.

Angle Tackle

This tackle is necessary when the ball carrier runs a wide play or gets close to the sideline. Coach your tacklers using these guidelines:

- Keep under control and be ready to move in any direction.
- Maintain a good balanced stance in a good hitting position.
- Drive your head in front of the ball carrier's number, across the line of his or her run.
- Drive your shoulder upward on the runner at about waist level.
- With your arms, grasp the runner behind the legs and lift him or her off the ground.
- Arch your back to lift and drive through the ball carrier.
- Keep the feet moving with short, choppy steps as you finish the tackle.

Figure 8.52   Proper tackling technique.

Open-Field Tackle

After the runner has cleared the line of scrimmage or when a receiver has caught the football and has just one player to beat, defensive players must make an open-field tackle. Coach your players that in the open field the most important thing to do is to get hold of the opponent and pull him or her to the ground. Stress these coaching points:

⊙ Keep under control with your legs bent.

⊙ Use the sideline to your advantage, penning in or getting an angle on the runner.

⊙ Remember that your number one priority is to grasp the runner.

⊙ Once you have a hold on the runner, help should soon arrive. But, if possible, try to drive the ball carrier out of bounds or pull him or her to the turf.

⊙ Don't worry about driving through the player or delivering a hard blow. Your sole responsibility is to get hold of the player and prevent the score.

Tackling Game

HEADS UP

Goal

To execute the proper form in tackling the ball carrier.

Description

Play 1 v 1 in an area 3 yards wide by 6 yards long. The ball carrier and the defender line up facing each other, with the defender on the "line of scrimmage," which is across the middle of the playing area, and the ball carrier at one end (see figure 8.53). The ball carrier's goal is to get past the defender and get to the other end of the playing area—in other words, gain three yards beyond the line of scrimmage. The defender's goal is to tackle the ball carrier, using proper form, before the ball carrier gains three yards.

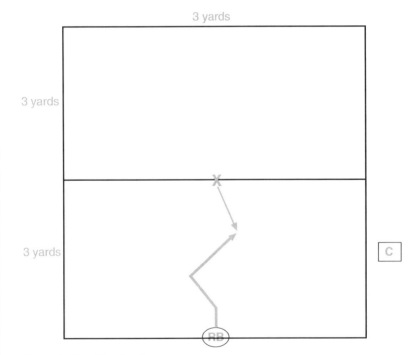

Figure 8.53 Heads Up.

The play begins on your command. Defenders get one point for keeping their heads up, one point for wrapping their arms around the ball carrier, one point for taking the ball carrier down, and two points for stopping the runner from gaining three yards. The ball carrier gets three points each time he or she gains three or more yards. Have the ball carrier run three times, then switch positions with the defender. Note: Before the players begin, do instruct them to keep their heads up as they attempt to tackle, and to slide their heads to the outside just before making contact.

To make the game easier:

- Make the ball carrier gain 5 yards before awarding the three points.
- Move the players closer together.

To make the game harder:

- Make the area wider.
- Move the players farther apart.
- Award the ball carrier three points for gaining any yardage.

Note: You can use this game for head-on tackling, and adapt it for angle and open-field tackling by making the playing area larger and placing the players differently.

Pulling the Flag or Touching

If you want to have a good defensive team in flag football, you must teach your defensive players to pull flags. In touch football, you must coach your players on the proper techniques of tagging a player. Players who learn the correct fundamentals of flag pulling and touching early can more easily develop skills as they get older.

Head-On Flag Pull or Touch

The head-on flag pull or touch is used when defensive players are lined up straight across from the offensive runner coming toward them. Defenders should keep low and center their attention on the runner's waist. Figure 8.54 illustrates proper flag-pulling technique. Figure 8.55 illustrates proper touching technique. Emphasize the following points to your flag pullers or touchers:

- Make sure that you are under control so as not to overrun the ball carrier or dive and miss the flag pull or touch.

Figure 8.54   Proper flag-pulling technique.

Figure 8.55   Proper touching technique.

- Maintain a wide balanced stance; keep the feet moving with choppy steps.
- Extend your arms and head in front of your body.
- Keep your head up, your back arched, and your knees slightly bent.
- Slide your body to one side to avoid contact and reach for the flag or touch the runner with two hands.

Angle Flag Pull or Touch

This flag pull or touch is necessary when the ball carrier runs a wide play or gets close to the sideline. Coach your defensive players using these guidelines:

- Keep under control and be ready to move in any direction.
- Maintain a good balanced stance and stay on your feet with your head up.
- Reach for the flag or touch the runner with your body under control, head up, eyes focused on the ball carrier's waist or numbers.
- Stay relaxed as you pull the flag or touch the ball carrier.

Open-Field Flag Pull or Touch

After the runner has cleared the line of scrimmage or when a receiver has caught the football and has just one player to beat, the defender must use the open-field flag pull or touch. Tell your players that in the open field the most important thing to do is get close enough to the ball carrier that they can pull the flag or touch him or her. Stress these coaching points:

- Keep under control with your legs bent.
- Keep your feet moving, head up, and arms away from your body.
- Use the sideline to your advantage, penning in or getting an angle on the runner.
- Remember that your sole responsibility is to prevent the score by pulling the flag or touching the runner.

Rushing the Passer

To improve the pass rush of the defensive line players, you can teach them the following techniques.

Bull Rush

A bull rush occurs when the defensive player gets control of the offensive blocker by locking his or her arms in the offensive blocker's armpits, and, with the leverage provided by locking his or her elbows, lifts the offensive line player up, forcing the blocker back into the quarterback. This type of rush requires good arm and hand strength.

Swim Technique

There are two ways to do the swim technique. One way is for the defender to move his or her forearm up and under the blocker's arm (see figure 8.56a) in an attempt to knock the blocker off balance. The other way is for the defender to extend his or her arm and swim over the top of the blocker (see figure 8.56b). Once the arm is over the blocker, the defender pushes off and moves toward the quarterback. Note that the swim motion and the pushoff should be one continuous movement.

Spin Technique

In the spin technique, the rusher uses his or her hands and arms to spin around the blocker and get into the offensive backfield (see figures 8.57a-b). In using this technique, the defender spins a full 360 degrees in getting around the blocker.

a

Figure 8.56 Swim technique.

b

Figure 8.56 *(continued)*

a

Figure 8.57 Spin technique.

(continued)

b

Figure 8.57   *(continued)*

Rushing the Passer Game

Try the game "Protecting the QB" that follows the Pass Protection Block section.

Covering Receivers

The defense must be able to cover the receivers to stop the offense from moving the ball through the air. Spend time training your players to defend the pass. Following are some of the necessary skills.

Proper Alignment

The defensive corners should line up 5 to 7 yards off the wide receivers. The safeties should line up 8 to 12 yards deep off the tight end or slot receiver. If you are playing only one safety, he or she should line up deep in the middle of the field.

Backpedal

Instruct your players to bend at the waist with a forward body lean. The backpedal should start with a step backward with the back foot and a push off the front foot. As players backpedal they should reach back with each step and pull their body over their feet. Their arms should move in a normal, relaxed running fashion. Players should be under control so when receivers make their breaks to catch the ball, the defenders are ready to drive on them.

Pass Coverage

The basic coverage in tackle football is man-to-man. This means that a defensive player is assigned to each offensive receiver wherever he or she goes. Figure 8.58 shows an example of man-to-man coverage in tackle football. Figure 8.59 shows an example of player-to-player coverage in flag and touch football. Use the following guidelines in teaching your players how to cover receivers:

- Keep your eyes focused primarily on the receiver you are covering (at the belt region).
- Maintain a 3- to 4-yard cushion between you and the receiver.
- Never turn your back on the receiver.
- Once the ball is in the air, play it aggressively.

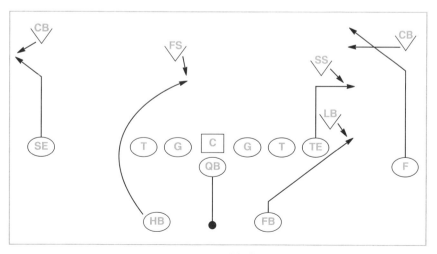

Figure 8.58   Man-to-man coverage in tackle football.

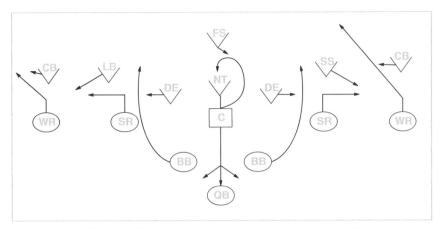

Figure 8.59 Player-to-player coverage in flag and touch football.

Zone Coverage

In flag and touch football, teams use zone coverage extensively because of the speed of the game and because flag and touch is 90 percent passing. A relatively inexperienced player can more easily learn the game and its techniques by playing zone rather than player to player. Use the following guidelines in teaching your players how to play a zone and cover receivers:

- Keep your eyes open and your head up to be alert for players running into your zone.
- Maintain a 3- or 4-yard cushion between you and the receiver.
- Never turn your back on the receiver.
- Once the ball is in the air, play it aggressively.

Covering Receivers Game

NO PASSING ZONE

Goal

To intercept the pass or not allow it to be completed.

Description

Play 3 v 2 or 4 v 3 in an area 10 yards wide by 40 yards long. The defense can play either player to player or zone. The quarterback begins with the ball on the offense's own "goal line" and signals the play to start (see figure 8.60). Receivers run straight down the field and run whatever pattern they want. The defensive backs backpedal and break to the ball when it is thrown. The defense gets two points for intercepting a pass and one point for preventing a receiver from catching the ball or causing a receiver to drop the ball. If an offensive player catches the ball, the defenders must tackle the ball carrier. After three plays, switch defense and offense, maintaining the same numbers on each side. If the offense is able to gain 40 yards or more within the three plays, any points gained by the defense are wiped out.

To make the game easier:

- Make the playing area longer.
- Play 3 v 3 or 3 v 4.

To make the game harder:

- Make the playing area shorter.

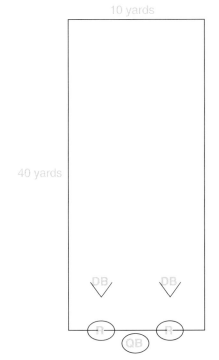

Figure 8.60   No Passing Zone.

chapter 9

Season Plans

Hopefully you've learned a lot from this book: what your responsibilities as a coach are, how to communicate well and provide for safety, how to use the games approach to teach and shape skills, and how to coach on game days. But game days make up only a portion of your season – you and your players will spend more time in practice than in competition. How well you conduct practices and prepare your players for competition will greatly affect both your and your players' enjoyment and success throughout the season.

In this chapter, then, we present a basic season plan that you can adapt for 8- to 14-year-olds. Use this plan as a guideline for conducting your practices. This plan is not the only way to approach your season, but it does present an appropriate teaching progression and a list of games that will help your players be introduced to, and practice, the appropriate tactics and skills. Remember to incorporate the games approach as you conduct your practices, using Game 1 to put your players in a game-like situation that introduces them to the main tactic or skill that you want them to learn that day. Then guide your players through a short question-and-answer session that leads to the skill practice. Here you should conduct one or two skill practices in which you will teach players the tactic or skill (or review the techniques if you've already taught the skill) and then conduct a fun drill for them to practice that skill. Remember to keep the introductions, demonstrations, and explanations of the tactics and skills brief. As the players practice, attend to individual players, guiding them with tips or with further demonstration.

We highly recommend having at least two coaches per team. If you do have two coaches, you can run two stations at the same time—meaning you could have two Game 1s going on at once, move on to two simultaneous Skill Practices, and follow that with two simultaneous Game 2s. Then rotate players between the two stations, so all players are introduced to, and practice, the tactics and skills for that day. For example, in practice 1 of the season plans, the main skills covered are tackling and covering receivers (see practice 1 below). While half your team goes through the tackling station games and skill practice, the other half could be going through the games and skill practice for covering receivers. When players complete their respective stations, they could switch stations and go through the games and skill practice for the other skill.

These season plans provide the purpose for each practice, the primary tactics and skills worked on in that practice, and the Game 1-Skill Practice-Game 2 progressions. Refer to chapter 5 for how to run a practice, including warm-ups and cool-downs. In chapter 8 you will find descriptions of all the tactics and skills, and games you can use to practice them. Throughout the season plans we refer you to the appropriate pages for those tactics and skills and games.

Good luck and good coaching!

Season Plans for 8- to 14-Year-Olds

Practice 1

- **Purpose:** To learn basic defensive concepts
- **Tactics and Skills:** Basic defensive positions and alignments; tackling (head on); covering receivers
- **Game 1:** Station 1—Heads Up (p. 158); Station 2—No Passing Zone (p. 166)
- **Skill Practice:** Station 1—Tackling (head on; p. 156); Station 2— Covering receivers (p. 164)
- **Game 2:** Station 1—Heads Up (p. 158); Station 2—No Passing Zone (p. 166)

Practice 2

- **Purpose:** To learn basic offensive concepts
- **Tactics and Skills:** Basic offensive positions and alignments; passing; catching
- **Game 1:** Station 1—Air Ball (p. 95); Station 2—Catching On (p. 140)
- **Skill Practice:** Station 1—Passing (p. 134); Station 2—Catching (p. 138)
- **Game 2:** Station 1—Air Ball (p. 95) or Screen Door (p. 128); Station 2—Catching On (p. 140)

Practice 3

- **Purpose:** To learn basic special teams concepts
- **Tactics and Skills:** Basic special teams positions and concepts; punting; kicking; covering punts and kickoffs
- **Game 1:** Station 1—Field Position (p. 144); Station 2—Kicking Into Gear (p. 151) or Trifecta (p. 148)
- **Skill Practice:** Station 1—Punting (head on; p. 142); Station 2—Kicking off or placekicking (p. 147)
- **Game 2:** Station 1—Field Position (p. 144); Station 2—Kicking Into Gear (p. 151) or Trifecta (p. 148)

Practice 4

- **Purpose:** To learn techniques for blocking
- **Tactics and Skills:** Blocking (drive and pass protection)
- **Game 1:** Station 1—Drive-Through (p. 118); Station 2—Protecting the QB (p. 123)
- **Skill Practice:** Station 1—Drive blocking (head on; p. 116); Station 2—Pass protection blocking (p. 121)
- **Game 2:** Station 1—Drive-Through (p. 118) or Hit the Hole (p. 100) or teach running play; Station 2—Protecting the QB (p. 123) or teach pass play

Practice 5

- **Purpose:** To learn to use blockers
- **Tactics and Skills:** Using blockers
- **Game 1:** Station 1—Follow the Leader (p. 130); Station 2—Screen Door (p. 128)

- **Skill Practice:** Station 1—Using blockers (head on; p. 131); Station 2—Using blockers (p. 131)
- **Game 2:** Station 1—Follow the Leader (p. 130) or The Escort (p. 120) or teach running play; Station 2—Screen Door (p. 128) or teach pass play

Practice 6

- **Purpose:** To learn to rush the passer
- **Tactics and Skills:** Rushing the passer; tackling
- **Game 1:** Station 1—Protecting the QB (p. 123); Station 2—Heads Up (p. 158)
- **Skill Practice:** Station 1—Rushing the passer (p. 161); Station 2—Tackling (downfield angle; p. 156)
- **Game 2:** Station 1—Protecting the QB (p. 123); Station 2—Heads Up (p. 158)

Practice 7

- **Purpose:** To practive effectively using blockers
- **Tactics and Skills:** Blocking (downfield; screen for flag and touch); using blockers
- **Game 1:** Station 1—The Escort (p. 120) or Screen Door (p. 128); Station 2—Hit the Hole (p. 100) or Drive-Through (p. 118)
- **Skill Practice:** Station 1—Downfield blocking (p. 119) or screen blocking; Station 2—Using blockers (p. 131)
- **Game 2:** Station 1—The Escort (p. 120) or Screen Door (p. 128); Station 2—Hit the Hole (p. 100) or Drive-Through (p. 118)

Practice 8

- **Purpose:** To learn how to play tough team defense
- **Tactics and Skills:** Pressure defense; contain defense
- **Game 1:** Station 1—Airtight D (p. 106); Station 2—Large and in Charge (p. 107)
- **Skill Practice:** Station 1—Pressure defense (p. 104); Station 2—Contain defense (p. 107)
- **Game 2:** Station 1—Airtight D (p. 106); Station 2—Large and in Charge (p. 107)

Practice 9

- **Purpose:** To develop the passing game
- **Tactics and Skills:** Passing; using blockers
- **Game 1:** Station 1—Air Ball (p. 95); Station 2—Follow the Leader (p. 130)
- **Skill Practice:** Station 1—Passing (p. 134); Station 2—Using blockers (p. 131)
- **Game 2:** Station 1—Air Ball (p. 95) or teach passing play; Station 2—Follow the Leader (p. 130) or teach running play

Practice 10

- **Purpose:** To practice effective pass defense
- **Tactics and Skills:** Rushing the passer; covering receivers
- **Game 1:** Station 1—Protecting the QB (p. 123); Station 2—No Passing Zone (p. 166)
- **Skill Practice:** Station 1—Rushing the passer (p. 161); Station 2—Covering receivers (p. 164)
- **Game 2:** Station 1—Protecting the QB (p. 123); Station 2—No Passing Zone (p. 166)

Practice 11

- **Purpose:** To practice using blockers
- **Tactics and Skills:** Using blockers; catching the ball
- **Game 1:** Station 1—Screen Door (p. 128); Station 2—Catching On (p. 140)
- **Skill Practice:** Station 1—Using blockers (p. 131); Station 2—Catching (p. 138)
- **Game 2:** Station 1—Screen Door (p. 128); Station 2—Catching On (p. 140)

Practice 12

- **Purpose:** To practice special teams concepts
- **Tactics and Skills:** Punting; kicking; covering punts and kickoffs
- **Game 1:** Station 1—Field Position (p. 144); Station 2—Kicking Into Gear (p. 151) or Trifecta (p. 148)

- **Skill Practice:** Station 1—Punting (p. 142); Station 2—Kicking off or placekicking (p. 147)
- **Game 2:** Station 1—Field Position (p. 144); Station 2—Kicking Into Gear (p. 151) or Trifecta (p. 148)

Practice 13

- **Purpose:** To develop the running game
- **Tactics and Skills:** Using blockers
- **Game 1:** Station 1—Hit the Hole (p. 100) or Drive-Through (p. 118); Station 2—The Escort (p. 120) or Screen Door (p. 128)
- **Skill Practice:** Station 1—Using blockers (p. 131); Station 2—Downfield blocking (p. 119) or screen blocking (p. 127)
- **Game 2:** Station 1—Hit the Hole (p. 100) or Drive-Through (p. 118); Station 2—The Escort (p. 120) or Screen Door (p. 128)

Practice 14

- **Purpose:** To practice effective pass defense
- **Tactics and Skills:** Rushing the passer; covering receivers
- **Game 1:** Station 1—Protecting the QB (p. 123); Station 2—No Passing Zone (p. 166)
- **Skill Practice:** Station 1—Rushing the passer (p. 161); Station 2—Covering receivers (p. 164)
- **Game 2:** Station 1—Protecting the QB (p. 123); Station 2—No Passing Zone (p. 166)

Injury Report

Name of athlete _____

Date _____

Time _____

First aider (name) _____

Cause of injury _____

_____

Type of injury _____

Anatomical area involved _____

Extent of injury _____

_____

_____

First aid administered _____

_____

_____

Other treatment administered _____

_____

_____

_____

Referral action _____

_____

_____

_____

_____

First aider (signature)

Emergency Information Card

Athlete's name _____ Age _____

Address _____

Phone _____ S.S.# _____

Sport _____

List two persons to contact in case of emergency:

Parent or guardian's name _____

Address _____

Home phone _____ Work phone _____

Second person's name _____

Address _____

Home phone _____ Work phone _____

Relationship to athlete _____

Insurance co. _____ Policy # _____

Physician's name _____ Phone _____

IMPORTANT

Is your child allergic to any drugs? _____ If so, what? _____

Does your child have any other allergies? (e.g., bee stings, dust) _____

Does your child have ____ asthma, ____ diabetes, or ____ epilepsy?

Is your child on any medication? _____ If so, what? _____

Does your child wear contacts? _____

Is there anything else we should know about your child's health or physical condition? If yes, please explain. _____

_____

_____

_____

_____

_____   _____
Signature   Date

Emergency Response Card

Information for emergency call
(Be prepared to give this information to the EMS dispatcher)

1. Location _____

    Street address _____

    City or town _____

    Directions (cross streets, landmarks, etc.) _____

    _____

    _____

2. Telephone number from which call is being made _____

3. Caller's name _____

4. What happened _____

    _____

    _____

    _____

    _____

    _____

5. How many persons injured _____

6. Condition of victim(s) _____

7. Help (first aid) being given _____

    _____

    _____

    _____

Note: Do not hang up first. Let the EMS dispatcher hang up first.

Provide excellent instruction to youth football players

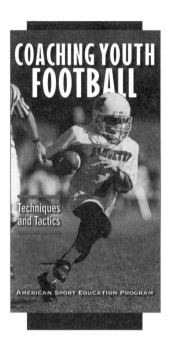

Tens of thousands of youth coaches have benefited from the *Coaching Youth Football* book. Now a new companion videotape will help you create an even more successful coaching experience. The *Coaching Youth Football Video* shows you how to teach the most important football techniques and tactics to your young players.

Approx. 30-minute video
ISBN 0-7360-3996-1

To learn more about ASEP, visit
www.asep.com

To place your order, U.S. customers call
TOLL FREE **1-800-747-4457**

Customers outside the U.S. should place orders using the appropriate telephone number/address in the front of this book.

HUMAN KINETICS
The Premier Publisher for Sports & Fitness
P.O. Box 5076 • Champaign, IL 61825-5076 USA
www.humankinetics.com

2335

6/01